Who Needs a Vagina?

Dear Susan

Enjoy

Love Steph

Who Needs a Vagina? (And While You're At It,
    Take the Kitchen, Too!)

Published in the United States of America by Legacy Projects

ISBN-13: 978-1986944182
ISBN-10: 1986944182

Edited by David Tabatsky
Cover and interior design by Bruce Kluger

Who Needs a Vagina?

...and while you're at it, take the kitchen, too!

A GUIDEBOOK FOR WOMEN, AGES 60 AND BEYOND

Gayle Israel

Legacy Projects

Contents

To be loved unconditionally from the day that you are born allows you to live a life that is full of promise. You ultimately make your own choices, but I believe that your light shines just a little brighter. That is what my parents gave to me. I dedicate this book to my mother and father who in my eyes are forever young, forever beautiful, and forever in my heart.

1 *Here We Go!*

Why am I in the kitchen? Who took my keys? What did I do yesterday, and who did I do it with? What did I eat? Did I turn on the dishwasher? Why would I? I never eat at home anymore! Is it hot in here or is it just me? Why am I sweating in February? Is there really life after menopause?

When exactly did maintenance become a full-time career—without vacation days or benefits (not to mention the cost), and when did my hair salon become my second home? When did bathing suit cover-ups become an essential part of my wardrobe? And how many colors do they come in?

By the way, have you seen my reading glasses? Most likely not! If you're reading this, you can't find my reading glasses because you probably can't find yours, either.

Well, isn't this a fun stage of our lives…

When the kids finally move out and the dog's dead, do you and your husband have anything to talk about, other than the kids and the dead dog?

Your secrets are totally safe with me! In fact, I won't remember any of them! Maybe a little amnesia isn't so bad after all. I know the exact year I was born. I just can't seem to recall what's happened since then.

How did I get here, anyway? Was I at the supermarket too long? Wasn't I just at a Mommy & Me class? When did my kids stop wearing braces? And who decided I was old enough to become a grandmother? A what? Who are you talking about? How is that possible? Can someone please identify this woman I'm looking at in the mirror?

Welcome to *Who Needs a Vagina? (And While You're At It, Take the Kitchen, Too!)*—my guidebook for women 60 and beyond.

It is not; I repeat *not* for the men in our life. The title alone will traumatize them. This is a reflective, humorous, heartfelt journey through the ages and stages of life, through the eyes of a 60-something year old woman.

I have been talking with my girlfriends about writing this book for a long time. Of course I can't remember exactly how long, and who I told what to, but what else is new? It's our "new normal."

It didn't happen overnight; that's for sure. I first started to write immediately after the birth of my first child. My journaling continued for many years and became a cathartic outlet to release all the intense feelings I was having—the deepest, darkest thoughts that were only meant for me.

Why couldn't women talk about their feelings? Why couldn't we be honest and talk about how sad and lonely we felt after having a baby? Were we so scared that it meant we didn't love our baby? No! It never had anything to do with that. It was the biggest change a woman will ever go through in her life, and everyone marched around as if everything couldn't be more perfect, while I knew it was far from it.

The changes in our lives were monumental, and they had brought with them emotions we had never experienced before. Of course, I loved my baby. I had never loved anyone more deeply, for God's sake! But nobody ever talked about these feelings. Back then, I felt like I was the only one having these thoughts, and at times I felt isolated, lonely, and sometimes even frightened. This was almost 35 years ago, and I believe it's different for women today. I certainly hope so.

Many years later, I found my journals, read them again, and placed them in the fireplace. I never wanted anyone who I loved to read them. They were only for me, and what I was going through at the time. Writing them helped me back then, and still, to this day, I encourage anyone going through a difficult time and struggling to see life clearly to write down his or her thoughts. Don't hold back! Then throw it away. I promise you that it will be cathartic. There are still times that I reach for my journal and most likely, I always will.

That got me thinking. I cannot be the only one with all these feelings about the changes we go through during our lifetime, and the need so many of us have to connect with each other so that our feelings can be validated and our voices heard. The changes we go through are too many to count, but through each and every chapter of our life, one thing is certain: we need each other.

We need to talk, and vent. We need a shoulder, a hug, a laugh, and most definitely a glass of wine!

Men are not void of feelings. They have strong feelings about certain things, such as the remote control, their cars, or the speakers that vibrate throughout the entire house. And let's not forget about golf! It seems like most men, not all, internalize their deepest feelings. I don't know if it's their wiring, their upbringing, or maybe both. It's hard for me to imagine my husband and his friends sitting around after a golf game discussing their "empty nest," asking if they look fat in their golf shorts, or finding out if they ever think about having work done on their face.

Shall I go on? I think, or I should say I know, that men are happiest when their last child is finally off the payroll. It's just different, not better; just different, and that is why our girlfriends are so important. Of course our husbands will listen—or pretend they are listening—and for the most part they do their best to understand, but they can't, and never will.

It's okay. Do you really care about the remote control? For us, it serves a purpose. For them, it's an intimate relationship. They need to know it's whereabouts at all times! Sometimes, they even try to "fix" our emotions. There is no "fixing." Women understand that about each other. We get it because that's just who we are.

After having worked as a mental health therapist for several years, I felt it was time to take a break. I never said I was retiring, but the mental health field is a challenging one, and after much soul searching, I knew I needed to recharge!

For the first time in as long as I can remember, I didn't have a schedule. I didn't have to be anywhere; no one was hungry, or needed to be picked up or dropped off; the dog was dead; the days of freezing on a soccer field were over, and I didn't have anyone's homework to finish, or help study for a test. I did so well up until sixth grade, but middle school math? Hello, tutors!

Some days, free of any obligations, I didn't even put on make-up, and of course those were the times I always ran into someone. I never said the word retire—ever. My husband used it all the time because I think although he would never admit it, he was slightly envious of my having the choice to do what I was doing. Or maybe he was afraid I would have more time for the "stores."

I understood. For me, I don't like the word "retire." So far, it's simply been a new chapter, and like all the other ones in our lives, it will not last forever. Our lives are changing each and every day, and none of us know what tomorrow may bring.

I still felt at my core that I wanted—and needed—to help people navigate their lives. For whatever reason, it is an ability that comes naturally to me. I am able to see situations clearly, where others may not be able to, and sometimes, with humor, lighten things up a bit. It is fulfilling when I can present a new perspective that helps to open someone's eyes so they don't feel sad or lost. I truly care about the people in my life and the obstacles and challenges we all encounter at some point.

Because I still felt this need, I had some inner conflicts. I was loving my freedom, and not willing to commit to another job, yet I wanted to share my insight and humor with women like me—women of "a certain age" who were probably experiencing most everything I was going through. Whether they, too, had become a mother-in-law, or were experiencing the ultimate pure joy of grandparenting, or had walked the long and excruciating path of saying good-by to their beloved mother or father, or helped their adult child rebuild their life after a divorce—we were all experiencing unchartered waters.

Some time ago, I was away with my girlfriends at a spa. After our massages, we decided to make appointments with a psychic. One girlfriend suggested that I ask the psychic about the book I was writing. All I can say is, it became a turning point for me.

I told her about myself, and the conflict I was feeling. She told me that I had the book in me and that writing it would be a way of sharing my insight, and hopefully helping in any way I could. Her words empowered me to continue my venture.

Each chapter is personal, directly from my life, and although we have all walked our own path, our fears, pain, tears, and laughter all come from a similar place deep in our hearts. That's just how most of us are wired.

So, girls, what do you think? Do we really still need a vagina? And the kitchen? I will get back to you on that one. (Can't those kids make the seder already?)

After a few drinks at dinner one evening with my mom, I asked her if she wanted to hear the title of my book. As the supportive, loving mom she's always been, she was excited, but as soon as I told her, there was dead silence. No reaction!

"So what's everyone having for dinner?" she said.

Well, this was awkward. We ordered dinner (and another drink) and still not a word. The next morning, my phone rang at eight a.m. I thought someone had died! It's a Jewish thing—if the phone rings that early, there has to be something wrong!

"You know I would never interfere in your life," my mom said, "but you need to change the title of your book. It's insulting, and disrespectful to your husband. And your father, too."

(Oy, she's bringing my father into this—the Jewish guilt!)

"Mom, this book has nothing to do with him. It's about women, and all the changes we go through."

The conversation ended somewhat abruptly, and it was clear that we did not see eye to eye. I felt deflated as I hung up because up until then I had been getting only positive feedback from everyone else. It still surprises me how much power a parent's words continue to have, no matter how old we are.

I immediately asked my husband to be totally honest and tell me if he felt disrespected in any way by the title. He promised that he didn't, and that was all I needed to know. In that moment, I realized that what was happening was not just a disagreement with my mom or that we didn't see eye to eye. It was bigger than that. It was about how differently her generation and mine viewed the world.

She came from a time when *nothing* was discussed, and today we discuss *everything,* and then some! I told Mom I respected her opinion, and always would, but that I hoped she could respect my way of expressing myself. I think she has gotten used to the title (sort of), although just recently she did ask me if my editor thought I should change it, and I told her he loved it!

My 31-year-old daughter asked if she could read my book, and while I wanted her to, I was slightly reluctant because I thought some of it would be impossible for her to understand or relate to at her age. She loved it, but asked me to explain the title.

Up until that point, there was no explanation needed. And that's when it became loud and clear that this book is definitely for women of "a certain age," the ones who immediately laughed when they heard the title and encouraged me to keep writing.

My daughter thought it sounded depressing, which is a normal reaction for a woman of her generation. It made me think back to when I needed to explain to her in an age-appropriate way where babies came from. The title, too, was age appropriate, and I told her that it was simply a metaphor for all the changes women experience after their children are born.

"From the moment you entered my world," I told her, "all that mattered was you. And now that you're on your own, you will always be more important than anything else. But it's also time to take care of what matters to me."

She looked at me, smiled, and said she understood.

"It's your turn."

So, getting back to you and me…it's so hard to stay focused, isn't it?

This book is about "us" and for "us."

So many changes, so much to talk about. And we love, love, love to talk—about anything and everything. We need to talk like we need oxygen. It's essential for our mental health and our need to be validated. We need to know it's okay to feel what we are feeling and that we are not crazy or neurotic (maybe a little). Well, if a little neurosis means being sensitive, caring, opinionated, smart, happy, sad, or lonely—so be it.

I know you understand. We are so overloaded with emotions that need to come out, and once they do, something miraculous happens because "it" is never as bad as we built it up to be. You know that's true. We are experts at building mental snowballs. We make something out of nothing. It's not a good day if there's nothing to worry about.

Stop it. You know you do it. We all do. It's in our DNA.

We ruminate. Then the poor husband makes the mistake of asking "what's wrong?" We reply "nothing," at which time I can only hope that at this point in my marriage he knows that "nothing" means "everything" and he's finally become the mind reader he claims he will never be!

You proceed to discuss what's bothering you and that's when they get that universal deer-in-the-headlights look, as in, "Now what did I do?" They don't mean it, and it's not intentional, but they just don't get it, or us—not now, not ever.

If you were feeling a little crazy before the conversation, you're probably feeling really insane, and be honest— pissed off! Maybe even like a paranoid schizophrenic, imagining things and hearing voices. Another good talk with the husband.

Digression: This book is not about or for our husbands, or for that matter *any* man in your life. I adore and cherish my husband of almost 40 years. I mean this with all my heart. He is a wonderful, kind, good man, a devoted husband, father, father-in-law, son-in-law, and grandfather, but I repeat, this book is *not* about or for our husbands!

This book is for us. Girls, you know who you are. We have a lot to say. We need to be heard and understood. We need to know that we are not crazy. After all, we are simply wired differently than men.

I know they wouldn't be interested in this book and wouldn't dare open it. After I write each chapter, I ask my husband if he wants to hear what I wrote, and he always says "sure." He listens, and to the best of his ability, pretends to be interested. That glazed over look must mean he needs a good night's sleep. I never feel insulted because I get it. At the end of the day, it's all about the effort.

Believe it or not, most of us are not recovering from an addiction or a life-altering traumatic event or sleeping with our best friend's husband. We have all had our own personal heartaches, and some are clearly much worse than others, but most of our lives are really quite ordinary.

This book is simply about the day-in and day-out of doing the best we can. It's about love, marriage, raising kids, friendships, losses, gains, and the transitions we have gone through as wives, mothers, sisters, and friends. We experience too many changes to count, but through each and every chapter of our lives, it feels as if women need each other more and more. In fact, girlfriends are crucial!

As a therapist, and within my own circle of friends, I listen every day to women striving to create "a new normal."

Although our children are adults, we continue to be enmeshed emotionally and physically in their lives, as well as with our grandchildren and our aging parents. We strive to maintain a healthy mind and a strong body, while nurturing relationships with our husbands and friends.

We all want our children's paths in life to flow as smoothly as possible, but we are learning to accept that we cannot take away their pain. As desperate as we are to ease their struggles, accepting that this is their journey and that we are simply along for the ride is most likely one of the most difficult challenges we face today.

To the best of our ability, we are helping our parents age with dignity and peace, hoping they are comfortable and enjoying a good quality of life. We are known as "baby boomers" and the "sandwich generation," but the truth is, quite often it feels more like we are a juggling act in the circus, struggling to keep those balls in the air.

There is much to be grateful for, and much to laugh at. I reflect on how I got here, while sharing my hopes and dreams for my second half. It's time to reframe our thinking, and if you haven't begun to do that, now is a good time to begin!

We need to delete the old recordings in our head and stop listening to the same old songs. Let's become mindful of how we speak—to ourselves and others—and respect the power behind every positive and negative thought.

I know that I am not the only woman who cannot leave the house without her magnifying glasses or struggling to say goodbye to the clothes in the closet from "another time." Who doesn't long for the days when we didn't have to work out or eat yogurt every day so our favorite jeans might fit? Make sure your hair appointments (and I don't just mean on your head!) are in place for the next "event" and the spanx are where they belong! I know that if I am going through all of this, so are you. I am not rich, not famous, and not that special! At the end of the day, it's not about a lousy deck of cards we may have been dealt; it's ultimately about how we "strategize " to play the game.

This book speaks to women who haven't always walked a smooth path, and anyone who says they have, well…

Watching the rich and famous may be are our guilty pleasures, but most of us are not famous, and never will be, and are probably not so rich, either! We are here, doing the best we can, finding balance and experiencing spiritual and personal growth, while learning to open up our hearts and minds to new adventures.

Let's not panic. Everyone please calm down. Of course you still need your vagina, perhaps not as much as before, but like I've said "that was then; this is now."

I know you agree on taking out the kitchen. Can't you imagine what a fantastic walk-in closet it could be? Let's be honest. How much longer are we going to continue to buy fruits and veggies that speak to us at the end of every week because we haven't looked at them once? Or, what about the leftovers we bring home from another restaurant that end up talking to the broccoli we haven't touched!

It's the beginning of our second act. We are choosing who will stay in our lives and who must go. We are ready to step outside the comfort zone, with a resiliency and inner strength we didn't even know we had. We have cherished and nurtured everyone else, and now, it's our turn.

It's time to give yourself permission to nurture yourself for a change. Let's work on not needing the approval of others for our self-worth. Can we finally let go of the way we *were* and embrace who we *are*?

We're not jumping ship; we're just learning how to steer our own. I don't know about you, but from now on I'm deciding who is in my second act and, oh, just one more thing—I really love sitting in the director's chair, and I am pretty sure you will, too.

So here we go, girlfriends…sit back, light a candle, and relax with a glass of wine. Relate to some or maybe all. Have a good laugh, a good cry, or hopefully both…

Much love,

Gayle

2 The Real Joy of Menopause

First of all, calm down. I can hear you from here, ranting and raving! Joy? What joy? The joy of having a sexy moustache? Or not being able to breathe in your favorite jeans? A closet filled with clothes that might fit, should fit, will never fit, sleeping, not sleeping, sweating, freezing— and those are the *good* days.

"Gayle, are you out of your mind?"

Of course I am, but it's not my fault. I blame it on menopause, and you can, too. Every woman I know does.

When I am not sweating to death, I could easily choke someone (usually the poor husband). Remember when you had a waist? Allow me to refresh your memory. It's the area around your stomach where a belt used to fit. I know I had one. It's just difficult to pinpoint what era and where it actually went, although I have a pretty good idea. I can't remember a lot of things I used to remember. Sometimes it comes to me about eight hours later and I shout out the information, and by that time, who the hell cares anymore?

It doesn't take a village to raise a child. It takes a village for me to finish a sentence. Conversations with friends go something like this: "You know, what's his name, he was in that movie with what's her name, you know, the one who looks like, oh come on, you know." At this point we are all just staring at each other. Okay, is anyone's brain functioning today? After about ten minutes of this extremely intelligent dialogue, we either give up or one of us miraculously figures it out.

Okay girls, who thinks a mustache is sexy, and let's not minimize the always enjoyable pattern of sleeping every other night! Sometimes you sleep, and sometimes you don't. Why do you think online shopping is so popular? Who buys bras at three a.m.? I do. They promised to make me look 20 pounds lighter and 20 years younger. What's the problem? Are you detecting a little delusional thinking? What do you expect, it's three in the morning! I'm thinking about starting an all-night Mahjong or Canasta game. Anyone interested?

I suppose things could be worse. I could be recorded snoring in my Victoria's (not so secret) pajamas! Have any of you lovely ladies taken up snoring (a feminine activity after menopause)? Yes, it's true. I didn't believe my husband, but he taped me snoring because he could not believe I slept through the sounds, the lovely, soothing sounds of a rhinoceros dying! OMG, what the hell was happening? Please don't be envious of such a romantic gesture because it's not appealing on any level! Now that we have a pattern of sleeping every other night, aren't we especially charming and fun to be with? Is anyone having fun so far? Raise your hand! Not so much! So get ready and let me tell you about "the real joys of menopause."

Since we don't remember anything any longer, I want you to go to the basement and find those photo albums from 100 years ago when you and your husband were dating. I said 100 years, calm down! You may want to have a glass of wine close by. Look how cute and thin you were, so in love with so much in common (at least you thought so!) Well, the way I see it, you and your husband have a great deal in common once again! I'm sensing some skepticism, so now would be a good time to bring the wine slightly closer and within your reach!

Try to remember when you used to shave your legs every couple of days, instead of months, and you would sometimes use your husband's razor. Let's stop pretending you had one of those fancy razors; we all used theirs. The good news is, since you both have a mustache, beard and sideburns you can now share razors, and he won't be angry because he may just have to borrow one from you. See how much better everything is looking so far? Drink up!

Since we have already discussed the "disappearing waist" situation, rather than feeling depressed about it (and who doesn't), let's try and look at things through a different lens. Although his jeans may be slightly tight on you, and yours are slightly big on him, you probably could start to share jeans. Neither one of you has a waist, and now the low-rise has become high-rise without anyone having to buy another pair of jeans. The savings are incredible. Cheers!

Okay, I admit it. I needed reading glasses first. Big deal! For a while there was some competition. I would be kind and offer my glasses if my husband's ego wasn't allowing him to see the menu.

"Noooo, these are *waaaaay* too strong for me," he said.

That remark made me feel like a blind bat!

"I can see the menu just fine."

Well, that didn't last long, and now we are both blind. He really doesn't look that bad in my leopard-trimmed readers. When did this happen? I never wore glasses my entire life. Now, I have about five pairs at the bottom of my pocketbook, and about 20 more scattered all over the house and car. If, God forbid, I leave the house without glasses I either have to turn around and get them or find a store to buy another pair.

It doesn't matter how much they cost; I can't see the price tag anyway. Again, I don't know exactly when all this happened, but who cares? It should be, and hopefully will be, the worst thing I will ever have to deal with when it comes to my health.

Look how much my husband and I have in common. We both can't see, and now we share our glasses! Come on, admit it, aren't you feeling warm and fuzzy? You didn't think you had anything in common anymore? Need a refill on that wine?

I probably don't need to revisit the facial hair situation, but let's just say that while our growth is increasing, theirs is decreasing. Do you think I am being insensitive with such a sensitive topic? I am merely attempting to point out (again) how much more we have in common than we realize. Neither one of us looks exactly like we used to, so maybe, just maybe, it's time to GET OVER YOURSELF! Believe me, I know that is certainly much easier said than done, but at least we can try to keep life in perspective, and not obsess. I'll drink to that!

As I was saying (I think), most of us don't exactly look like we used to or eat like we used to—or drink like we used to, for that matter. When my husband and I were dating, I would pick at everything. For a year and a half while attempting to be cute and thin, I was really starving to death! I had to make sure I wasn't going to lose this "nice Jewish boy" who my parents had sent me to college to meet!

Stop pretending you weren't there for the same reason. Today, things are different, but back then, it was a hunt for a "nice Jewish boy—the marrying kind."

Allow me to digress. One of my favorite stories about my mom comes from when I was dating my future husband. At the time, he was living in the basement of his aunt and uncle's house after college. Every night, he would come to my house and my mother would use her beautiful crystal and silver tray to serve the "potential husband" coffee and his favorite cake. This went on for nine months. We became engaged, and the very next night, we were still sitting on the same couch we had been occupying that entire time. Only this time, the lights were off in the kitchen. The crystal was back in the closet and no cake was in sight.

"Where is the coffee and cake?" my fiancé said.

From my parent's bedroom in back of the house we heard my mother scream.

"Get it yourself! It's in the kitchen!"

I guess she felt her work was done, that it was "mission accomplished." We still laugh at that story almost 40 years later.

Where was I? Oh right, I was being cute and thin, but starving. We got married, and one day, the poor guy tried to take one of my French fries. Now don't forget I hadn't eaten in a year and a half. You would have been aggressive, too! It wasn't my fault, and it wasn't my finest moment. I am exaggerating, but I know you get it.

Now, our appetites are quite equal. Like needing glasses, I cannot exactly pinpoint when all of this happened, but we do have that in common now, too. I am not happy about it, just stating what is! Just when you thought you've heard enough about how much we have in common, there's one more thing that is bringing the two of you closer together. Your circle of friends starts to change. Along with all of our physical and mental changes, friendships vary as well. We begin to see things differently in some of the people who have been in our lives for a long time.

Sometimes friendships were formed because of our children's needs, or through work, or life can bring you together with people because that is what is supposed to be happening at that particular time of your life.

Then your needs change. Life happens. There are no fights or disagreements. Life just seems to pull you into different directions, and if we listen carefully to our inner voices we begin to understand who we need in our life. Less is more, and for many husbands, that was always true.

Stop pretending he was allowed to have his own friends. They tried desperately to hang onto those college friends, the ones you hated, but when you were dating not only were you being cute and thin; you also made believe you loved his friends. Well, along with not sharing my French fries, we also had to get rid of the friends. I was so busy in those days making all of those changes! After slowly eliminating the college friends, my friends became his friends and life was good.

These days, it seems less is more. I want to be with people who make me happy, bring out the best in me, and accept me for who I am. It's time for you to decide who to keep and who to let go.

This, my friends, is my perspective on the "the real joys of menopause."

Obviously I am trying to find the humor at a time that is often not so funny. For many of us it is a time when we may need to reach out for some professional help. This is not a sign of weakness, but one of strength and intelligence. Just like anything else we cannot control, much of this is more about our attitude than anything else, and it is something we can eventually control. We may just "choose" not to, for whatever reason. It's not always easy to have a positive attitude. Some days, we are better at it than others. For myself, the support of my family and my "chosen" friends help me make it through the storms of my life.

Hopefully we are learning to view ourselves through a different lens right now, and letting go of the way we once were. Laughter will always be the most powerful medicine, and figuring out how to not take ourselves too seriously helps to ease anxiety and stress so that we can live a longer, more peaceful life.

If you can't eliminate toxic people from your life, creating healthy boundaries is the next best thing. Finding humor at a time like this can be challenging, but we must understand and accept that most everything that happens to us is all about the attitude we "choose" to have.

And one more thing: My new best friend Pinot Grigio has been quite helpful. Have you had the pleasure of getting to know him?

3 It's 10 p.m.— Do You Know Where Your Children Are?

Raising children is not an easy task by any stretch of the imagination. We would probably have been better off not knowing what was ahead of us. My mother used to refer to that time as the "war zone years." Slightly on the harsh side, but certainly some truth to how she described a family battlefield. I think I prefer "the good, the bad and the ugly." The stages, phases, laughter, tears, joys, and sorrows all determine the dance of a family, the dynamics of siblings, sleepless nights, proud moments (some not so much), broken hearts, milestones, and memories—some forever and always…

It is almost impossible to remember when I didn't have children. I can barely remember my college years when I met my husband and the years we spent BK (before kids, not Burger King). I have wonderful memories about that time, but it seems like another lifetime. Some feel there's luck involved while raising children, and who they become. I believe luck is about health, and everything else is about blood, sweat, and tears. We survive, and hopefully they thrive.

Daniel was nearly two when we moved into our first and only home. He was a wild stallion in those days, so we built a fence to coral our gorgeous boy. If anyone wanted to spend time with us, we were in our backyard! Warren and I thought we lived in a castle. I had never dreamed we would live in such a beautiful home. Everything was just perfect! Thirty-two years later, the house is unrecognizable. I don't live in the past or have regrets, but there was something about those hungry years. Everything tasted a little bit sweeter. Gratitude came easier, even though we have much more now. I suppose it's human nature to take what you have for granted until it's no longer there.

We were the new kids on a block I never imagined I would live on. Our neighbors across had a little boy Daniel's age and a beautiful four-year-old daughter. We became instant friends. I'm pretty sure that I invited ourselves over to help them decorate their Christmas tree and we've been going there ever since, which adds up to a lot of tree decorating for a nice Jewish girl!

They go to church and we go to temple. That's the only difference I can see, though their food might be a little better. I've loved sharing our joys, sorrows, and celebrations through the years. We have continued to be there for each other ever since we first met, and I'm sure we always will.

Mr. and Mrs. Rose lived next to us, and they had grown children and grandchildren. They seemed old and cranky to a 28-year-old. They pretended to like us, but Daniel always ran onto their lawn, throwing rocks or making mischief and the Roses always had that make-believe "Oh, he's so adorable" face, when I knew they wished I would lock him in our house.

Now, guess who has slowly morphed into Mr. and Mrs. Rose? We have! We are grandparents, and we've become old and cranky, just like them.

But wait a minute. Wasn't it me on the corner with all the other moms, waiting for the school bus? Wasn't it me teaching my kids how to ride a bike or getting them on to the day camp bus, not knowing if I should cry because they were growing up or scream with joy to have some "me" time? Yes, it was. That's why I love seeing all those children now, running and playing. I reminisce for a moment but trust me; I don't long to be there again. These are simply warm memories from a long time ago.

I wonder if all the neighborhood kids think of Warren and I as Mr. and Mrs. Rose. Funny, I don't feel as old as I am. Do you? I bet those kids think that's just who we are. Maybe that's just the circle of life, but it's *our* circle and I love it.

And then one day, something miraculous and totally unexpected happened, a transition I never saw coming. I can't pinpoint exactly when, but one day, my adult children began hanging out with us, and not because we forced them to. Now, we sit around the fire, laughing, drinking wine, planning vacations, and loving our time together. There's no fighting, no tears, no slamming doors, no cursing (and those were the good times!) We've become friends and they just happen to be our children.

It was never something I could have envisioned during the "good, bad, and ugly" years. I knew, or should say I hoped, that the tough times would pass, and prayed that they would be okay. What I truly could not know was that my children would become adults who make my world, and the rest of it, a better place.

As time marches on, there's much more to these new dynamics. It's also become about letting go of them and being quiet. Always coming from a place of love and the best of intentions, learning to let go has probably been one of the more difficult challenges of being a mom. There will always be a part of us that when we look at our children, no matter how old they are, or how tall they get, or even when they become parents themselves, all we see is our little girl or little boy, who we want to protect with all our might. We will always want to smooth the waters and put out any fires for the rest of our days, but we must learn to accept their choices and know that taking away your child's pain is not possible. It is their life and their journey.

If we want to continue having a wonderful relationship then I suggest beginning by working on ourselves and not our children. We did that already, remember? I am *trying* to be a better listener. I am *trying* to keep my opinions to myself. I am *trying* to let them fly. Sometimes, I feel scared because the unknown can be frightening, but I *try* to have confidence and faith that hopefully we have given our children the right tools and guidance to enable them to make decisions that work for *them*, not us.

Please don't misunderstand what I am saying. Being a mom is first and forever, and as difficult as it may be sometimes, their decisions and choices are theirs. We may not agree, or see it the way they do, but they are adults now making their way in this complicated world, just like we once did and are continuing to do. It's okay if you still see them in their footy pajamas. I believe there's a part of us that always will, but try to the best of your ability to keep it to yourself! Reflect back on how you felt when your parents made a "loving" comment. Try and let them be. It is the best gift we can give to our new best friends and hopefully they will always want to hang out with us, especially when there's good food, wine (and your wallet).

We all want our children's lives to go as smoothly as possible, but we cannot take away their pain. They will fall and tumble. They will struggle, but we must remember that they are on their own journeys, making mistakes, just like we did. Having faith and confidence will empower them long after we are no longer here. Becoming a better listener rather than a better talker will make for healthy, happy relationships with your children and whoever they bring home. Be patient, stay calm, and allow them to develop at their own pace. Guide them quietly and they will become who they were meant to be.

4 It's My Turn...

I was told quite often that when your youngest child finally goes off to college, and your beloved dog is no longer with you, a glimmer of light begins to shine at the end of the child-rearing tunnel. You may even have some time and money to shop for another pair of black shoes.

Please don't misunderstand me or take this the wrong way. Children and dogs are wonderful and fulfilling (most of the time), however, I really don't think I need to go into details or explain myself, do I? I know I don't because we—and you know who I mean when I say we—understand the endless effort that goes into raising a family as well as walking and feeding the dog, the one that every child promised they would be responsible for. And just tell me who has a better life than a Jewish dog, anyway? I thought *my* grooming cost a lot! Enough said.

Why is it that whenever women need to express their feelings, they first preface a sentence with, "It's not that I don't love and adore my children or my husband...?"

I know that. Everyone knows that. Why are we always apologizing for something? Enough already! Stop it! You did an amazing job!

My youngest was off to college, and so was I—back to

graduate school at 50 to become a therapist. I decorated a room for myself and wasn't interested in how anyone felt about my color choice. I started planning some adult vacations without worrying who was swimming with the dolphins and if there were chicken fingers on the menu.

My beautiful untrained Bichon was not with us any longer and that long and winding road was starting to turn in my direction, meaning the light at the end of the tunnel was beginning to shine just a little brighter…until…

My dad, my wonderful loving, caring, warm, devoted, supportive father was slowly slipping away from us. My family, especially my mom, didn't give it a name, but the truth is, no one really had to. My dad was struggling, and too proud and too scared to complain. He probably didn't want to bother anyone, and he never did. He never burdened any of us and never had a single enemy ever. His purpose in life was to make people laugh and feel good. His was the voice of reason. It was excruciating year after year, month after month, day after day, to watch my dad slip away. It doesn't seem to matter how old or how strong you think you are. There were days when my intellect ruled the day and I would close my eyes and try to hear his voice and envision what he would say. His words and wisdom had always guided our family through any blinding snowstorm. I had so much more than most. My sense of humor, my inner strength, my self-confidence and, hopefully, some wisdom, were gifts from him. Gifts of a lifetime.

I have wanted to write about my father since that day, Thursday, January 8, 2009, when I was sure our lives would never be the same. Thoughts would race through my mind constantly but I wasn't ready to put them on paper. It was still too painful for me. The reality of his loss was too much. I wasn't able to speak about him or think about him without crying and I would look at pictures and think to myself, where did he go? I still expected him to walk into my house through the front door and give me a big bear hug and tell me how beautiful I looked. No one loved his family more than my dad. All of us, and I mean, two son-in-laws, a daughter-in-law and six grandchildren, always knew how much they were loved and cared about. There wasn't a day that my dad didn't tell you that he loved you or how great you look, and that he was so proud of what you were doing, whatever that might have been. Each and every one of us had his or her own personal cheerleader in my dad. Just imagine a world where every child had someone like that on their side, rooting them on.

He is always in my thoughts. For a long time, no one would or could talk about what was happening to him. To us. We hoped and prayed that he was just being forgetful because he was getting older. We blamed his inability to focus on bad eyesight. We prayed that the cataract surgery would be the answer to help him read a newspaper, see a movie, or watch television. Eventually, he was no longer able to do any of those simple things. We continued to make excuses because denial was safe. It was too painful. We blamed his triple bypass for possibly cutting off circulation to the brain. We were all so desperate to find answers and reasons but mostly we wanted a miracle. Still, none of us, my brother, sister, or my mother, would say the word.

His decline continued for several years. My mother worked so hard to keep their life as normal as possible. She protected him fiercely, and for the rest of my days I will always admire her strength, courage, devotion, and love for her life partner. She desperately clung to their life like a raft in the middle of the ocean, but the gaping hole could never be repaired.

We finally started to say it: Alzheimer's. My dad had Alzheimer's. We were able to say it before my mother could. It took her a long time to say the word in referring to her husband and the father of her children. How exactly does a spouse come to terms and accept the mental deterioration of their partner for 57 years? Perhaps if you don't say something out loud, it's not really happening. It will go away. He will get better. But it *was* happening, and we all began to finally deal with the reality of what was affecting all of us. Day by day, we were slowly losing the captain of our ship. That is what Alzheimer's does.

I know he fought hard. I didn't know where he went. His body was strong, but his mind was not. He was in and out of psychiatric hospitals for the last six months of his life, experiencing agitation and sundowning. We took turns at his bedside, hoping and praying, hanging onto every word, still imagining a miracle. Every night, driving home, I would cry, still not able to accept what was happening. It seemed that for my whole life, I was comforting someone else. I always had more than most, until then.

The days were long, with constant phone calls and the fear of hearing the phone ring. We all hung on tight until that day, Thursday, January 8, 2009, when my beloved father made the decision that it was time. I know he decided because nothing, absolutely nothing my father did, said, or felt was without intent.

I never could have imagined it, but today I can talk about my dad, and write about him without crying. I will always yearn for his wisdom and words of encouragement, but most days I can close my eyes and hear his words and his wisdom deep in my heart and soul. Most important, I can still feel all the love he had for me, which will remain with me for the rest of my days.

5 Girlfriends

My girlfriends have always been a huge part of my life. As far back as elementary school, I can remember my best friend and the things we used to do together. Mostly, I remember we were always giggling. What happened to giggling? It's still the best medicine.

When I think back to my childhood girlfriends, they were all so very different, and I loved them all because of that. I just didn't know that back then. When we were young, we weren't overthinking, overanalyzing, and oversharing every aspect of our lives. We were just trying to get through third grade!

I realize now that the girls I was having fun with and sharing secrets with was a result of the chemistry between us. That was all that seemed to matter, then and now. I knew who I wanted to be with. There was the friend who I giggled with, the friend who I felt grown up with, and another who I trusted my secrets with. No friendship was the same, but I got something that I needed from each and every one of them. The only difference now is that we have the ability to recognize who we need in our life, why we need them, and who we also need to let go of.

I had never envisioned myself married to a "traveling

salesman," but that was the path intended for me. Most of the years spent raising my children I did alone. My parents were a huge support system, and although my mom was working when my children were young, she was always there for emotional support as well as just coming over after work to give me a break.

My girlfriends helped with the details of my life, and it was all about the details when we were raising our children. Yet, I still needed to figure out how to reinvent myself after growing up in a family where my dad was home every night at seven p.m. and Mom cooked practically every night. I knew it was a Tuesday because I smelled meatloaf in the oven. That was my model of family life and probably yours, too, with or without the meatloaf.

The 1950's and 60's was the era of *I love Lucy*, *Leave it to Beaver*, and *The Donna Reed Show*. When I reminisce with friends about growing up during that era, it seems like we all had the same dinners, the same snacks, and watched the same television shows. There was not an abundance of choices like today. Sushi wasn't part of the English language and no one I knew was counting grams of fat. If you lived on Long Island, Green Acres Shopping Mall was the place to be, and on Sundays (if you were Jewish) it was a law that you had to have Chinese food. Swanson TV dinners were a treat we enjoyed sitting in front of the television with only four stations and our biggest challenge was getting off the couch to change the channel. Can you imagine?

It was a time when most moms were home and fathers provided the income. That was my only model of family life. Years later, while married with two young children, Tuesdays were no longer meatloaf day and Dad wasn't coming home right on the dot at seven. We weren't sitting down to a family dinner, and in fact most nights he was not coming home. It was my two kids and me.

Okay, now what? What the heck do I do with myself and two kids all day and night besides have a nervous breakdown? I knew I had to do something, but what? It was lonely most of the time and quite overwhelming—a difficult time in my life and for our marriage, mostly because I didn't have anyone to help me through those times of insanity, when I was overwhelmed and exhausted with the responsibilities of being a mother. At the end of any long day, after staying home with children or working outside the home, everyone needed a break.

Stop it right now! Do not for a minute tell me you didn't feel there were times that you might have been losing your mind when your children were young. I felt so envious of my friends whose husbands were home. Although now they admit they are envious of me that my husband travels. Is anyone happy?

I was never a particularly independent girl. I grew up dependent on my mom and dad, going from college to getting married. I hardly knew anyone who wasn't going down that path. That's the way it was. So I, Ms. Dependent, forced to reinvent herself into an independent, stronger version of who she was. I knew that is exactly what I needed to do. I just didn't know quite how to do it. My toolbox was empty.

I began to need my girlfriends, I mean really need them, and not just for playgroups and lunches at the diner, but to help me navigate my journey towards an independent life. I began to understand that asking for help was not a sign of weakness but more of an awakening that people were willing to be there for me, and I just needed to ask. But like anything in our lives that needs to change, it certainly doesn't happen overnight. It became clear to me that I loved my husband and the life we were building, but I needed to develop a separate life from him, too. I came to understand and accept that being married didn't mean that it was his responsibility to fulfill every emotional need that I had. This was *my* life, and although he was my partner he was not responsible for my happiness. The *only* person responsible for my happiness was, and is, *me*. My husband was not going to fill any voids I felt. That was for me to figure out.

Enter girlfriends, and my road to independence.

As our lives evolve and change, one thing seems to never change. As important as my girlfriends have always been, as I get older they have become even more so. Perhaps as we age, we become wiser in choosing who we want to be with, and because of that our friendships feel deeper, richer, and more fulfilling than ever before.

When we were younger and raising our children, most of our friendships, and the people we spent a great deal of time with, were connected with our children and their happiness. We made friendships through playgroups or in our neighborhoods. Whatever was best for my kids was always my priority and I believe most women do the best they can in that department.

Some women went back to work, while I made the choice to stay home and felt fortunate to do so. It was a personal choice, but for some, working outside the home is a financial necessity, or for others it is a personal choice. In a perfect world, my wish is that women could support each of our individual choices, and not undermine each other. Sometimes, we judge others so quickly without ever walking a minute in the shoes of the person we are judging.

Live and let live. There is absolutely no right or wrong, even though we all know women who can do no wrong! The perfect wife, the perfect life—the one whose life has been perfect every step of the way, the one who left the hospital after giving birth in her jeans, the one whose baby slept through the night as soon as they brought them home from the hospital, the one who never needed a pacifier (we needed as many as we could get), the one whose child snacked on broccoli, while mine ate Doritos for breakfast, the one who toilet trained himself before his first birthday or the brilliant, gifted child who was reading to his friends at his second birthday.

Let's never forget the lovely teenage years when their child didn't experiment with alcohol or God knows what else. And if you don't mind, I'd rather not discuss the high school years when it was time to apply for college. Enough said about "the perfect child," because he or she does not exist!

I am developing post-traumatic stress right now just talking about this stuff! Sorry, I digress. It's impossible to stay focused! Where was I? Oh yes, my girlfriends…

Whatever world you found yourself in, your girlfriends were the people who you had things in common with and as our children got older, everyone' needs started to change once again. Your children started to make their own friends, had their own opinions, and gradually certain friendships began to fade away.

Here we go again, another transition.

As women, doesn't it sometimes seem our lives have been one big transition after another? I feel like I could break into a song from *Fiddler on the Roof.*

"Transition…Transition!"

Some people have lifelong friends—from elementary school, sleep-away camp, high school, or college. Friends with history are special friends in a separate category. They knew your parents, siblings, and the house you grew up in. It was such an innocent time. Even though you probably don't see each other that much, and maybe if you met each other today you might not be friends, but nothing is quite like being with a friend who knew you from another time. It will always remain a unique relationship, no matter how much time passes by or the distance between you. That just never seems to matter.

My dad always loved to hear about my friends and was always interested in the details and the drama. And with girls, there was always drama.

"Honey," my dad would say, "your friends are just like a

meal. Some are great for a drink or two, and say goodnight. Others, a drink and dinner, maybe even dessert! Some, it's just coffee at the diner."

I am sure you get it. It's up to you to figure out who is worth your time, and how much of it, if any at all. At this point of our lives, it's quality, not quantity. Less is more. We all have so many people in our lives. It is up to us to decide who, what and where; don't you agree? Some people are better seen two times a year. It's not a bad thing. It is what it is. It's learning balance and boundaries, to place people where they belong.

I don't know about you, but my girlfriends are more important to me now than ever before. That's because by now we've all become filled with infinite wisdom, and are able to recognize the strengths and weaknesses in each and every girlfriend and accept them as I hope they embrace me.

Of course there are times we become frustrated and disappointed with each other because our expectations are unrealistic. We sometimes try and mold each other into what and/or who we think we need them to be and do not accept the limitations we all have. When we learn to be aware of our own needs, and understand who in our lives can fulfill them, then our relationships can be more meaningful and life will surely be more peaceful.

It is difficult to admit our own flaws and insecurities. We all have them, and when we look deep within ourselves and be honest, we can begin to understand why we have chosen to be with certain people. That will also help us realize when it is time to let go of those who do not belong in our lives any longer.

When I reflect back on the people who have come in and out of my life, I realize why they were there in the first place. They were supposed to be there. I also understand why others have come and gone. Different people become part of different chapters of our lives.

Friendships, like any relationship, require nurturing, patience, and acceptance. Getting older has its challenges, and even though I cannot be without my reading glasses, there are certain things that are crystal clear. Toxic people are just not welcome any longer. Red flag alert! When people show you who they are the first time, believe them! We all know people like this, and now is as good a time as any to say "Bye bye!"

I love my friends. They are my support system. They are my cheerleaders when I need encouragement. They are my shoulder to cry on when I need one and their glasses are always filled to celebrate anything and everything. We shop, eat, see movies, play canasta and Mahjong, read books, play golf, travel, and go to the beach. We laugh, cry, share secrets, and most important, we share our lives.

My friends, and you know who you are, have been an essential and huge part of my journey and have helped me become who I am today. Those friends I may not see all that often, or friends I no longer see for no other reason than life has moved us down different paths, have still contributed to my story and created memories that will remain etched in my heart for the rest of my days.

6 The Art of Accessorizing

Hello, my name is Gayle, and I love to shop.

Every couple of days my car drives itself to another store. I suppose I could try and take some responsibility for my behavior and not blame my car but that is not how I see the situation. I have very little self-control. Warren and I have never seen eye to eye on this. Girls, I know you get it! What's wrong with him, anyway?

Let's face it; none of us were born with a closet filled with black shoes. I still don't know what the big hoopla was over Imelda Marcos. She liked her shoes, so if the shoe fits, find out immediately what other colors it comes in—although I'm still not convinced there is any other color besides black.

There is absolutely no joy in shopping if I can't afford to buy something. Some girls are okay with that. They like to look. I like to carry shopping bags. To each his own!

What's better than the thrill of the hunt and finding a great sale?

Warren says I never bought anything that wasn't on sale. I think that's when I started using the trunk of my car as an armoire. It's worked out much better because I just couldn't take the shopping interrogation any longer.

As I have gotten older (and who hasn't), clothes don't always look like they used to, at least not on me. All right, I'm being kind. For most of my life that was my obsession—how I looked, and I'm sure that, for many women, that still continues. For me, it was a constant roller coaster of weight watching, food, feeling great, feeling horrible, self-loathing, and constant negative self-talk. The scale determined what kind of day I was going to have. This went on and on for what has seemed to be my entire life. I was either on a diet or off a diet. I either felt good about myself or felt bad about myself. Life was black and white, which was a very destructive and toxic way to live.

I can't say exactly when I began to see things differently. My thought process began changing in my 60's and it definitely has not happened overnight, that's for sure, and I know I am not alone. If I am transforming my thinking at this point in my life, I have to believe other women are as well, or trying to figure out how.

There's a name for what is happening to us now and I call it freedom—*mental* freedom, to be more specific.

Please do not misunderstand me. Of course I care about my emotional and physical well-being. I still care very much about my appearance. I rarely leave the house without make up and I love clothes, but what has changed dramatically is how I see myself and what I say to myself in response. Life has become grey, and many shades of it, with very little black and white. I do not feel horrible about myself anymore, and if I find myself resorting to my old habits of self-criticism, I just stop. I cannot keep the negative thoughts from entering my mind, but I do have the power now to determine what I do with these thoughts and how long I allow them to linger.

We can choose to allow negativity to escalate, which only lowers our self-esteem, or we can make a conscious decision to have a positive conversation with ourselves and keep up our confidence and self-esteem.

As I've gotten older, I've come to understand that I now have the mental freedom to choose how I see myself and not be concerned with how I think others perceive me. When I was younger, what the outside world thought seemed so important. What your parents thought, your friends, your neighbors, your boss—could it get any more exhausting? Now, I care about what I think is important and what I want.

I realize that sounds completely narcissistic, so please let me clarify. I simply don't obsess anymore. I do the best I can. Of course I could exercise more, drink less, and make better food choices, but the difference now is that I am trying, not obsessing.

I've decided that I lived that way long enough, and I am not going to live the second half of my life obsessing about my thighs. I will not allow the scale determine if I am going to have a good day. I try to see each day as the new day it is. Cliché or not, yesterday really is gone.

I continue to be a work in progress. We all are. I am not that special! You need to become conscious of your thoughts and the old recordings in your head that have been playing the same song for quite some time—as in forever! I am definitely not 100 percent there yet, but I have come to accept that I never will be because that would mean I am a machine, not a human being—and machines don't buy shoes!

When you become conscious of your thoughts and what you say to yourself, you realize you are usually your own worst enemy. Would you ever speak to a friend the way you speak to yourself? I hope not! Try to encourage yourself. Place the focus on your strengths and minimize your weakness, instead of the other way around. Understand that there will be setbacks. I experience them all the time. Sometimes, I revert back to my old negative thinking and the same old song. The major difference now is that I am choosing not to allow the negativity to escalate and control me. Most of the time I am in control.

Perhaps awareness and perspective come with getting older. My dad would tell us that life was like climbing a mountain. The views would be forever changing with each step you took. Many women I know are unhappy about getting older. It's difficult for some to accept where they are in life. I never minimize their feelings. It is how they feel and I always try to validate them.

For me, I love this time of my life. Do I look like I used to or have the same energy I used to have? No, I do not, but what I love now is the mental freedom. Okay, I absolutely cannot be without my reading glasses because without them everything important, like menus and price tags, are blurry.

Maybe the perspective we have now is like having a pair of invisible glasses that help guide us to see life more clearly and to understand what and who truly matter. Of course aging has challenges, but let's look at our glass half full. Don't you want to finally come to peace with who you are—not who you were—and be with who you want to be with and enjoy them for who they are now?

You don't have to love everything and if you're like me you have no problem finding something to kvetch about on a daily basis, but I love the peace and clarity at this time of our lives. We've earned it. It's been a long road, raising our children, taking care of our parents, and continuing to do so.

I live a more tranquil existence now, which means it's time to come to peace with our parents, accepting and understanding that they did the best they could. No matter what has happened in our past, it's time to stop blaming and making excuses. We didn't have choices as children, but as adults, we choose how to live, and at the end of the day, isn't peace of mind what we are all trying to achieve?

It's time to reframe your thinking, and if you haven't begun, start now! Be receptive and open-minded to new ideas and adventures, whatever they may be. It is so easy and comfortable to do the "same old, same old." Move away from your comfort zone and step outside the box. It really only hurts for a minute...

Whatever path you have taken is okay. It's where you were supposed to go to get where you are now. It's time now to enjoy having the confidence and freedom to choose whatever it is that will bring fulfillment and peace into your life. I really don't know when that little black dress turned into a not so little black cover up, but I'm okay with it, at least most of the time!

If I choose to buy another pair of black shoes because—well, just because I want to, and the shoe size is the only size that hasn't changed in 30 years, just leave me alone, and please do not ask me how many shoes a woman really needs!

7 Maintenance (and I Don't Mean Your Car)

Unless you have come to terms with your grey hair, muffin top, and some particularly sexy facial hair, just stick with the plan! After all, what choice do we have?

Where exactly does one begin? Hair, mani, pedi, facials, waxing, spanx, yoga, Pilates, personal trainers—oy! I'm sure I missed something! Are you exhausted yet? I don't know about you but I could use a nice long nap!

Does all of this maintenance sometimes feel like a runaway train? Perhaps a full-time job, without benefits or a vacation? Thank God I stopped working because maintaining myself has become my new career. I can barely get out of the house on some days. Every time I turn around there's more grey than I care to discuss and I'm back in that chair. It's become my second home!

Manicures and pedicures are just a given. Facials are optional, at least for me, because when I had one recently the girl doing the facial asked me an innocent question, which turned out to be more than I bargained for.

"So what have you been using on your skin?"

I told her whatever I was using at the time, thinking my

47

skin had been looking pretty good, so I expected a nice answer from her.

"I don't think it's working for you any longer."

This was supposed to be calming and relaxing? I was so annoyed.

Just do your job and stop selling products!

Of course when the facial was over I bought everything she said I needed. A moment of weakness. What is wrong with us?

We are at a wonderful time in our lives now. Our friends' children are getting engaged, married, and having babies. It's hard to wrap my mind around all this. Some of those children walking down the aisle are the ones we watched on soccer fields, at Little League, or at those precious ballet recitals where the little girls were all kicking in different directions and picking their noses at the same time. All weddings are beautiful, but those, with children you've known for so long, are especially meaningful.

Whoever decided that wedding invitations should go out eight to ten weeks before the wedding really knew what they were doing. It had to be a woman. We need that much time to prepare for the wedding, and I am not talking about my own child's wedding. I'm just a guest at these other ones, but what will I wear? What will fit me that week? Who else is invited? I can't wear the same dress if the same people will be there. When do I need to do my color? Where are my spanx, which I now refer to as short-term, non-invasive, relatively inexpensive liposuction. And don't forget make-up appointments, and the mani and pedi, and I'll skip the facial this time if you don't mind.

I need to digress for a moment.

Even though we've been married a long time, I had no choice but to make an executive decision. My husband is no longer allowed in the room while I am getting ready for a wedding, until of course I need help zipping the dress that I am praying still fits! He left me no option on this.

Recently, we were getting ready for a wedding—well, let's just say I was getting ready and I took the panty hose out of the package. We all know that when you take them out they look similar to feet pajamas for a nine-month old!

My husband thought he was funny and said "And those are fitting who?"

I was exhausted and sweating, and that's when I made the decision that he needs to get dressed in another part of the house—maybe the backyard—so I can begin my own private "dance of the pantyhose." Girls, you know the moves, where you jump around the room until they're finally where they are supposed to be! Then, if you are having spanx surgery—well, let's just say breathing will not be an option for that evening!

Do you want to look good or do you want to breathe? You cannot do both, sorry. Those days are long gone.

You're already totally exhausted and you haven't even left the house or danced in those gorgeous shoes that will make you want to cut your feet off by the end of the evening. How much fun are we having? Let's not discuss how during this entire ordeal your husband is just about getting into the shower—after he has napped, of course— while you've been getting ready for what, the past eight to ten weeks, ever since you got that invitation.

Now he's in the shower, but you need him to come back in the room, and yes, he has permission to enter because you need him to zip up your dress. Prepare yourself: another warm and fuzzy moment is about to take place. He starts to zip, and let's just say it's not moving up as smoothly as you would have hoped, and that was after eating yogurt all week. It's just so unfair!

I start to hear some unpleasant groaning and breathing, and then he says something which he will pay for at a future date.

"When did this fit you?"

OMG!

"Listen darling, the noises and comments must stop immediately, just zip it, and I mean the mouth and the dress!"

Finally, you have transformed yourself and everything is in place. He gives a little spritz under the arm after his nap and puts on a tuxedo. Seems pretty fair and equal, don't you think? Obviously, things are not getting easier, but what is your alternative—grey hair, a muffin top, and a sexy mustache? Oh well, enough said.

Off we go to another wonderful evening of sharing the excitement and celebrating this beautiful young couple who are about to begin their lives together, filled with hopes and dreams for "happily ever after."

We find our seats, the crowd quiets down, and the ceremony begins. I take my husband's hand. Sitting next to him during each of these ceremonies, I become nostalgic and reflect back to the time when we were those two young people, and for that fleeting moment, we still are. For that moment, it is just us, and he looks so handsome in his tuxedo and I can't remember what we fought about on the way to the wedding. I look at him and think to myself, I would say yes again. Yes, I would do it all over, again and again and again. And even though I won't let him get dressed in the same room as me, I am confident he feels exactly the same way I do.

8 Learning to Play Golf

Warren's travel schedule left little time for extracurricular activities other than those with the family. When he was home, he was a great, hands-on, devoted, and loving dad. Everything he did was always for his family, and never himself. His career path has been challenging for all of us, but it has always provided us with a wonderful life. Although he was away quite often while our children were young, his relationship with them always remained strong. He might not have been here for the homework, the baths, and the "occasional mouse in the house," but he never ever missed the highlights of their lives. We all had to make sacrifices, but who doesn't? His strength of character and commitment to his family was what we all knew and felt—then and now!

Once a year, Warren would attend a golf outing for business, and due to his constant work, his golf skills were nonexistent. Every time he came home from this outing, he was mortified about his lack of ability on the golf course. I suppose he just couldn't take the embarrassment any longer and decided to try a few lessons before the next outing so that, maybe, he could land a ball on the fairway and not in the woods.

He had only intended to learn a few skills and never anticipated he'd enjoy golfing as much as he did. He slowly became hooked, which I'm sure any man or woman who plays golf regularly can understand. So he started taking more lessons. And then *many* more lessons. He set up a stupid green felt thing in the basement where he would practice putting. He was definitely on the verge of becoming obsessed, which I had only heard about from others, but never understood what people were carrying on about.

I still don't really understand it! While he was obsessing, putting away in the basement, I had absolutely no interest. It was not appealing to me. I had been a tennis player most of my life and didn't feel the need for a new sport. I was happy for him to have an outside interest, other than ceramic tile! The poor guy spends half his life in airports, so I knew it was great for him to finally have an outlet of his own, as long as he left me out of it!

I don't have to tell you that the "golf bug" grew larger and larger. We decided to join a golf club where he could play more, and meet people at his level. For the first time in our married life, he had more friends than me. I thought the camaraderie was great.

Just one question: How does a man spend four hours in a small cart, eat lunch, keep score, and not know everything about that person? When he came home I would ask him all about his partner's wife, kids, and career. Warren always told me he didn't know, that it never came up! Can you imagine?

As he continued to enjoy his new golf life, he continued talking about all the people he was meeting and that golf is very social and many couples play together. He told me I would love it! I told him I was happy for him but really not interested.

Being the amazing salesman that he is, he convinced me to take a few lessons. I figured, how difficult could it possibly be to hit a stupid little ball?

It's really, really, really hard to hit the stupid little ball!

I could not hit the goddamn ball. This was ridiculous! I really didn't like it. In fact, I hated it and didn't want to do it.

"I told you I wasn't interested. Leave me *aloooooone*, thank you very much!"

Warren wouldn't give up on me. He took me out for the first time to play nine holes. After the first one, where I had to hit the ball like 82 times (at least that's what it felt like), I was exhausted and frustrated. I didn't know if I needed a drink or a nap—or both. Where were the snacks, anyway?

"You know those couples you told me about who were laughing and having fun, I haven't seen any."

I just wanted to go home.

"Shut up and get in the cart!"

I just stared at him with that "I am going to kill you very shortly" look. He told me to shut up and I was ready to impale him with my driver! Was this what all the other couples were doing? Awesome.

"Stick with selling tile!"

After I flung my five-wood across the green, he told me to relax in the cart, and to "be quiet." I was too tired to argue. Another warm and fuzzy afternoon spent together. The future was looking grim. Warren finished the nine holes, and I drove the cart. Thank God I could do something fairly well.

I hate when this happens, but he ended up being right. I was noticing many couples playing golf together, and actually having fun. Granted, I wasn't in the cart with them, but I did hear some laughing.

I spent that entire summer taking golf lessons and practicing, only playing with Warren. He stopped telling me to shut up and get in the cart, and I stopped having the urge to stab him with my driver. I will admit the Bloody Mary's eased my frustration a little. The future was looking brighter!

Little by little, I stopped hating it, and eventually I didn't have to hit the ball so many times, and actually really loved being out in the fresh air. These days, I refer to my golf game as "Sybil plays golf." I never know who will be showing up that day, but the good news is, I don't really care. I enjoy being with my girlfriends and other couples, laughing, never taking any of this too seriously, and enjoying a gorgeous day at a magnificent country club.

I will never be a great golfer, but it's not that important. Don't get me wrong, I'm proud of myself that I've improved and learned something new later in my life, but what I enjoy most is that Warren and I can share this experience at this time of our lives. God willing, as we grow older, we will still have the gift of good health to keep playing together for many more years.

I must thank my husband for pushing me, encouraging me, having confidence in me, and not taking 'no' for an answer. This is the first time in our marriage that he pushed me instead of the other way around. It's usually the woman who pushes, who plans, and creates the life a couple enjoys. This was all his doing, and so far it's working out pretty well. I just hope he doesn't take up another sport, because like I told him before, I'm really not interested.

I feel very grateful! Oh, and one more thing, for you "new golfers "and us "not so new golfers," Bloody Mary's are definitely the way to go!

9 *Dinner with Daniel*

My son was never a baby. Of course he looked like a baby but Daniel never acted like one. He hated all baby things and cried everywhere—in the stroller, the high chair, the crib, the car seat, and even in the playpen. He was only happy when he was running and free. For the first few years of his life, we had a fenced-in backyard.

Fortunately for him, Daniel was handsome and funny, which helped us get through those "baby years." He was probably around three or four years old when the crying finally quieted down, but he didn't become a toddler, either. He was always an "old soul" who made me laugh all the time. The boy had shtick! His sister, Jessica, was a pretty serious baby, but when her brother was around, he always made her giggle. He loved to make her laugh then, and still does today.

While other three-year olds in nursery school were busy with their crayons and blocks, Daniel hung out with the teachers, and they loved him. Everyone loved Daniel. You couldn't help it. He has the likability gene. Throughout his school years, every teacher conference was the same.

"Daniel is a charming, funny young man, but he needs to save the jokes for the playground."

They wanted to be mad, but it's hard to be mad at someone when they are making you laugh!

When Warren traveled, Daniel became the "man of the house." It was a pretty big responsibility he took upon himself at 10 years old. He would check the windows, asked me if I set the alarm, and even took the garbage out. Back then, I thought it was so mature of him. Now, when I think of that, it makes me feel sad that he felt that burden of responsibility at such a young age. Then again, I guess that's who he was—never a boy, always a man—except for the exceptionally lovely and memorable teenage years!

It seemed that right after his Bar Mitzvah an alien moved into the house. I never saw the spaceship land, but Daniel was no longer the funny, charming, and mature young man that had been living here. I can't say I wasn't warned, as we all were about the teenage years, but until you're in it you really can't imagine how crazy it can be.

Some of you may have experienced those lovely, warm and fuzzy family dinners when no one was talking to each other. Maybe I'm exaggerating because I did hear a grunt every now and then, before we heard doors slamming and sibling battles. Who could ever forget our memorable family vacation to California when I wanted to leave my son on the Golden Gate Bridge? I particularly looked forward to the daily morning phone call from the attendance office, asking if Daniel was coming to school today.

"Yes, as soon as I drag his ass out of bed!"

Such fond memories of the teenage years. I still don't think I have recovered from teaching him how to drive! Looking back, that must have been the time when one glass of wine just wasn't enough!

However challenging that period was, getting your first-born ready for college was very emotional. A part of you can't wait to zip up his suitcase, and another part can't believe you are actually zipping up his suitcase. These "firsts" are fraught with so many emotions, which come with the territory.

So off to college my first-born went. I sat on his bed and had myself a good cry. I know most of you did the same thing and felt the same way. Our husbands—not so much. The financial burden was too overwhelming. I understood that, but our emotions ruled the day. Who needed him, anyway, sitting next to me while I was sobbing? I was a blubbering, emotional mom, staring at his Little League trophies. Sometimes, you just need to be alone.

So guess who came to dinner for Thanksgiving—my charming, funny, old Daniel. Don't get me wrong; he had his share of drama during the college years, but he was back. All that I knew and cared about was that the boy I once knew was back.

How can you know as a mom what will happen to your children when they go away from you? You worry so much about their well-being, and wonder if what they are going through is permanent or just a phase. Of course now I have perspective, but at the time, when you have to begin the process of letting go of your children, it can feel like you are on a tightrope without a net. We blame ourselves for everything, and question if maybe we could have done things differently.

Did I say too much or too little?

Was I strong enough, or too strong?

Could I have been a better mother?

When our children are growing, our maternal instincts are all that we have. No one is perfect, but I know in my heart I did the best I could. Things happen that are out of our control and sometimes we second-guess ourselves. After all, aren't we responsible for the well-being of this child we brought into this world?

They mature and develop on their own clock, not yours. We need to be patient, which is hard and can be frightening. We have expectations, and sometimes compare their lives to what ours were at their age, which is unfair to them, and to us. We were raised in a different time, by two different people. It's natural to think about that, but it isn't realistic or even terribly helpful.

Then it happens. Your little boy becomes a man—not a little boy *trying* to be a man, but a real man who has matured in his own time to become who he was meant to be. He still is charming, funny, smart, and handsome, and that's who he always was. I just needed to chill out a little more. I know it's easy for me to say it now, but I'm just happy that I can.

The phone rings. It's Daniel. Sometimes my heart drops just a little when he calls me. I think it's a mom thing, always and forever worrying about something.

"Mom, are you around Thursday night for dinner?"

"Of course, honey, I'd love to have dinner with you."

Warren had been away that particular week, and I was having a small pity party. Most of the time I'm okay, but sometimes it still gets lonely.

I met Daniel for dinner, just the two of us, which rarely happens. We talked, we laughed, and had a wonderful evening. I didn't feel lonely anymore.

What is it about those boys that, from the minute they enter your world, they continually tug at your heartstrings? Mothers and sons are so different from mothers and daughters. We think we raise them the same way but we really don't. It's not possible. Even though they both eventually leave you, daughters never really do. The boys leave and you know they are gone, but it seems there has always been an invisible thread that keeps us emotionally connected, no matter what.

I got home that night and started thinking about my dinner with Daniel. Of course I love and adore him, he's my son, but you just can't know how they are going to turn out. You hope and pray for a good outcome, and that night was it. I sat across the table from my son, but also the man he has become, and I loved being with him. He is a wonderful, caring, thoughtful human being and still really funny.

Accepting our children for who they are, respecting their judgment and decisions, embracing their strengths, and minimizing their weaknesses is the only way we can maintain healthy and happy relationships with them.

Be patient. One day your son, "your grown son" will call—not with a problem, but for a dinner date. And, yes, you too will drop everything to sit across the table from the amazing man he has become.

10 *My Daughter, My Friend*

My mother admitted to me after my daughter was born that she prayed during my entire pregnancy that I would have a girl. Daniel was her first grandchild, and while I was exploding with emotions I never knew existed, even the second time around, her preference didn't matter to me at all. I actually thought I was having another boy because I couldn't imagine myself with anything other than a boy. Now, as my daughter has matured and grown into an incredible young woman, I can understand why my mother prayed for me to have a daughter.

As I have gotten older, I have also come to understand so much more about my relationship with my own mother. When you are younger, you only have the ability to see life through your own eyes. Your compassion and empathetic skills have not quite developed. Some of us never develop those skills, but now I see my mom not just as my mother, but as a woman, just like me. Of course we are different, but we've walked a similar path—one she paved and showed me how to handle. Her family has always been her priority. She taught me to not harbor negative feelings and to walk away and let go of expectations. I didn't always agree with her when I was younger, but she felt so strongly that nothing was worth going to war over because the consequences would be devastating to the family. Once again, my mother was right!

She is older now, although I do refer to her as Benjamin Button. She has slowed down a little, but not mentally at all. She's smart, sharp, looks amazing, keeps up with current events, and now, at 86, she is in the process of reinventing herself, since her companion, Kappy, passed away. I know they loved each other and cared deeply for one another and that isn't easy for me to acknowledge. I was always happy for them, but since my dad died it has been difficult to think of my mom with another man. But it was a special time for both of them.

When you are not living near your family any longer, a strong dependency develops for your partner. There are no children to raise, certainly not as many expenses, and it is just the two of you, enjoying life once again after so much pain and sorrow. Now, my mom is learning how to be alone and not feel lonely. I don't know what tomorrow will bring, and she swears she will never have another boyfriend.

Stay tuned . .

Nearly 32 years ago, my daughter nestled into my heart and has been there ever since. When the nurse first brought her to me, she placed her gently on my chest. Only hours old, she nuzzled her way right into my neck so that our faces could touch each other. I remember back then thinking that she was the sweetest little thing, and she still is.

Oh, don't get me wrong! Having a daughter is not always a bed of roses. Does the expression, "Save the drama for your mama" ring a bell?

You bring this beautiful baby girl into the world and your mind is overflowing with all kinds of visions and expectations of what having a daughter will be like. The cute pigtails with pretty little pink bows, playing with her dolls, dress-up, skipping off to kindergarten holding hands with her best friend, giggling with her girlfriends, the awkward years of braces, sleepovers, her first crush, first boyfriend, first break-up, the proms, college years, and of course, your little girl in her wedding gown!

Everybody calm down. That's *your* vision.

As it turns out, this beautiful, precious little person who you gave birth to is actually quite different than you. What? How is this possible? She doesn't like what I like? She doesn't see things the way I do? She has her own sense of style and doesn't like what I think looks good on her? She actually has her own opinions?

Well, it's time to get over yourself because it's not all about you! Your daughter is her very own person, with her own ideas, visions, style and opinions. I think it has taken me this long to fully understand this, embrace it, and admire and respect the woman she has become.

I was extremely fortunate to be born into a family with parents who loved and cherished everything about me. I was close with both my mother and father, and shared a great deal of my life with them, and continued to do so into my adult life. I thought I shared almost everything with my mom until I had my own daughter, and realized how little I shared with them.

I am still not sure which is better, under-share or over-share. I know we are referred to as the helicopter generation because we "hover." I understand it because I am a reformed hoverer. Why do we need to hover in the first place? Is it for us or them? When and why did we become so enmeshed in our children's lives? Is it best for them or us? Are we so controlling that we feel the need to control their lives—even into adulthood? Do we think our way is the only way?

My daughter was a quiet, peaceful child who needed down time while finding her place in this world. She became a vegetarian at the age of eight. I thought she might have been switched at birth, because I never met a burger I didn't like. A vegetarian? What am I supposed to do with a vegetarian? I knew how to make chicken cutlets and meatloaf.

She would remove a bug from the house and bring it outside so it could be free and find its "family." Me? I had no problem stepping on it. Are you sure you're my child?

One Christmas, we spent the day with family in the city. It was a brutally cold, blustery day and we saw a homeless man on the frigid concrete, wrapped in a garbage bag. Jessica took off her gloves and put them in his bag. She was only nine years old. Her heart remains the same today.

I never was a quiet person who needed downtime. I prefer to be in the mix. She likes it too, but on a limited basis. We've always been different that way. Back then, I couldn't see that. I could only see what I needed her to be. There were times I felt frustrated and couldn't understand why she wasn't like me or needed what I needed. My husband helped me open my eyes and understand that as complicated as I made it, it was really simple.

"She is not you!"

I still remember his words almost 20 years later. Four simple but powerful words!

When you have a son, it is easier and natural to separate yourself. You love and cherish your son and daughter equally, but it is not about that. Aside from the obvious physical differences, you also know that one day your son is probably going to leave you for someone else. It's natural. However, I never had those thoughts about my daughter leaving for someone else. It doesn't happen. Of course, you hope that one day they have their own life, but your daughter, emotionally speaking, never ever leaves.

Girls, let's be honest, it won't be your son who has those tweezers ready when you're in the home—another good reason to mind your own business when you become a mother-in-law! Your daughter-in-law could be the one responsible for your senior grooming. *Oy vey!*

When we have a daughter, the process of separating ourselves from them is not conscious. We are both girls and have all the same parts. We want to be close to them, and relate and understand them. How is it possible that they can become so different from us? For goodness sake, we gave birth to them! The nerve of them to want and need to be their own person!

At the end of the day, we do not have any choice but to let go and allow our daughters to become who they were meant to be. Some women continue to hover and perhaps they always will. Maybe that works for their daughters, as well, I don't know, and it is none of my business to judge what works for others.

I could easily have remained a hovering mom because I was one—once upon a time. I tried hard, but my daughter wouldn't have it, and now I admire her independence. It only took me about 60 years to get to where she already is. She lets me in on what's important to her, or what she needs to tell me—not what I need to know. I've learned to respect her decision-making. I am learning to be a better listener, not a better talker. I work hard at giving her advice only when she asks, and even then I try to be sensitive to her needs, not mine.

Our relationship is special to me, not because she is anything like me, but because of who she has become in spite of my hovering. I love her quiet strength. It's so powerful.

When you are raising your children you love them with all you have, and the inevitable separation is difficult, but by letting go of them they emerge into the people we never imagine, and that's a beautiful thing.

I suppose it just comes with the territory. We will always be their mother and want to take care of them, but they are flying solo now, and we are simply along for the ride! Don't forget your wallet!

I know now why my mother prayed for me to have a

daughter. Even though my mom lives in Florida, we share our lives, even if it's over the phone. Jessica and I share our lives, too. I could never have dreamed my little vegetarian (yes, she still is) would become my dearest friend. We still are really different, but none of that matters. We get each other. We laugh and giggle at all the same things.

During those awkward years of braces, heartaches, and insecurities, my dad would always reassure me.

"You just wait. Your little girl is going to turn into the most beautiful butterfly you've ever seen."

To this day, I still don't know how he could possibly have known, but that is exactly what has happened, inside and out.

11 *Becoming a Mother-in-Law*

Speaking of minding your own business, my mom told me almost 40 ago, when she first became a mother-in-law, that she decided it was also the time to have plastic surgery. I thought, okay, the kids are finally married (thank God) and now it's her turn to spend some money on herself—maybe a facelift, collagen, Botox, whatever! No, you're wrong, just like I was! She proceeded to tell me about a zipper surgically implanted into her lips, which was supposed to help her "zip it!"

Throughout the years, there have been many times I have disagreed with her. I am a firm believer in airing your feelings. My mom would stick to her belief that nothing is worth going to war over, and it's important to move on from things that have been said or done that make you feel bad or hurt your feelings. I would listen to what she had to say, but I still didn't agree—until I became a mother-in-law!

I hate it when my mother's right!

Becoming a mother-in-law is a new role that nothing quite prepares you for. Being a daughter, sister, wife, and mother is not a dress rehearsal for dealing with a new married couple, building their own lives together, suddenly entering your life. It requires new skills, like learning how to mind my own business (MMOB) and accepting things I cannot change and keeping my mouth shut (KMMS).

After all these years, I'm starting to understand my mother better, as I come to realize that you need to let go of what you think is the right way, or worse than that, make comparisons of how you did things! My advice (not that anyone asked) is that unless you feel something is going to be a disaster—MMOB and KMMS!

No one is saying this is easy. This will remain a life-long challenge, and not a bad one, because it's all worth it!

We all have had role models in our lives, some obviously better than others. Those are the cards dealt to us, and with some wisdom and clarity as we get older we can pick and choose which behavior we would like to emulate, and be conscious of those that cause us problems.

My parents had two sons-in-law and one daughter-in-law, and they had phenomenal relationships with each one of them. I am not naïve to think that there were times when they saw or heard things that made them unhappy, but you never heard a word. They would vent to each other but never interfere. I couldn't believe they both had so much self-control. They were always supportive and encouraging, provided a shoulder to cry on, and were mostly so much fun to be around. They were wonderful parents to share our lives with, never interfering and always guiding us gently through difficult times while celebrating every occasion they could. These memories will last all of us a lifetime. I hope my children and their spouses will feel the same as I do about my mom and dad.

The wasted minutes, hours, and days, worrying if we said the wrong thing or if we didn't do what they wanted—it's just crazy to do that. It's (almost) never about us. Everyone has his or her own agenda. We come from different places and are just trying to survive in this world, with no intention of hurting anyone. Their behavior is not personal. It's all about them, not you!

And just for the record, I haven't yet totally ruled out the zipper plastic surgery. I always like to keep my options open.

12 *Becoming Mimi*

What is wrong with lollipops for lunch? Cookies and milk for dinner while watching television? As a grandmother, this works for me. Still in a diaper? So are lots of people. (They just don't talk about it!) I love to watch television and eat dinner. Oy! Our children have become parents and now their rules have rules.

Mimi (that's me) to the rescue!

My little muffin came into my life nearly three years ago and my life will never be the same! Anyone with a grandchild may attempt to explain what it's like, but they can't do it. No one can, because there is no way to describe all of these new emotions. I suppose there are some similarities to when you had your first child because it's such a new experience. But as much as you loved your children and your heart was exploding, this is a tsunami of emotions! If you're a grandparent, you know exactly what I am talking about.

It takes time to process and embrace what is actually happening. Watching your child take on the most awesome challenge of their life is simply breathtaking. They stumble and they fall, and they get up and do it all over again, just like we did, but it's their turn now. We always want to smooth the waters for them, but it's their journey into parenthood. We are right beside them, probably hovering, but hold your tongue. Zip it!

I never want to strip away their confidence by jumping on everything just because I may feel things should be done differently. Who said our way was the right way? Don't forget the mantra, "I had my turn!" As difficult as it is to watch your children struggle, they must work through the joy and pain. There is no other way.

I get to do the fun stuff. I kind of feel like I earned it. I also know that absolutely nothing happens to them if they skip dinner, have a lollipop for lunch, watch a little too much television and are not toilet trained by a certain age. Everyone eventually loses the bottle and pacifier along with the diaper.

Part of the joy of being "Mimi" is not sweating the small stuff. I did that already. But that's what parents do and always will. It's okay, but for me, I zip it up and encourage them to keep doing what they are doing.

Thousands of books have been written about becoming a grandparent and every yenta maven wants to offer their opinion, which of course they think is the only one. But forget about your books, the internet, and the yentas. Just like that day when your first child was born, when your first grandchild enters this world, you will be changed forever. The joy is immeasurable. That child has the power to make the rest of the world disappear. They take away every ache and pain, and make my life better in every way possible, and each stage has been better than the next.

When my daughter was pregnant with our second grandchild, the same fear surfaced when I was pregnant with her 30 years ago. Would I be able to love another child like I love my first? It didn't seem possible, but when the second was born I could feel my heart expanding and exploding once again. My little angel boy Ethan just melts my heart. Nothing is more beautiful than when two people bring a child into this world. It's overwhelming, scary, and uncharted territory, but they are a family now and their lives will never be the same—and neither will mine.

As a baby, Ethan has a little time before he will be having lollipops for lunch, but I am confident that Sloane will show him the way. She knows just where to look for those lollipops, and for the rest of my days Sloane and Ethan can have anything they want!

Mimi just can't say no and she never will…

My Sloaney girl,

You are only four and a half years old and I don't exactly know when you will read this, but I need to tell you how I feel about you.

Your mom and dad were not able to stay married and that's okay, but you are the most incredible little girl I have ever known. You are so young but you are an old soul. Your kindness, your sweetness, and your intellect are amazing and you have brought all of us so much joy. I always knew you would show us the way. When your mom and dad split up, I worried about you so much. They weren't meant to be. Who knows why? Sometimes, we look for answers and there aren't any. I am your Mimi, and as long as I live, that is who I will be. You are so special to me and you and I are so connected. It's hard to explain, but we just are and I know we will always be. As you grow, I will be by your side. There may be obstacles beyond my control, but one day you will be able to make your own decisions. I love you so much and want you to know that my heart will always be with you, no matter what happens and wherever you may go.

All my love forever,

Mimi

13 Becoming Parents to Our Parents

My sister, brother and I met at my parent's apartment to finally empty it out. After two years of gentle discussions with my mom about why Florida was the best place for her to reside, it finally happened. Thank God it didn't take long to sell her apartment because as long as she had one in New York, she would keep coming back for the summer season, as she and my dad did for 20-something years as snowbirds.

She would say over and over again that, "my family is here," which was true, but like many people do as they get older, much of their memory focuses on yesterday, when the grandchildren were young, and our family had Sunday night dinners. There were years and years of that, and as wonderful as it was, that was then and this is now.

Since my dad was no longer with her, my mom knew that she could no longer afford both homes and she was emotionally paralyzed, which seemed quite understandable. We slowly helped her make that difficult decision, and I wouldn't let up because I knew this was where she needed to be at this time of her life.

She tried to keep busy, but the loneliness was a slow death. Kappy, her wonderful companion, and someone who watched over her, lived in Florida. He still drove and had hair, so one could only imagine how many casseroles were waiting to knock his door down! For many reasons, Mom needed to reside in Florida.

It has been more than three years since my dad is gone. It feels so good to be able to talk about him, laugh, and remember his infinite wisdom and boundless love without crying. You couldn't have paid me enough money to imagine I could feel this way, but I do.

When we met to close Mom's apartment, I parked the car but I could not get out. A crushing wave of emotion came over me that I was not expecting. Perhaps it's impossible to prepare for these uncharted waters. I thought I had come such a long way and was so much stronger, confident that I could deal with whatever I had to. I was wrong. I just sat in my car and cried. I knew my brother and sister were waiting for me, but I just couldn't move. Still crying, I got out of the car and walked towards the building where my parents lived together for 15 years after they sold the home they lived in for 40 years. I walked past the pool where my kids would swim and where my parents would talk to everyone, because that's who they were—the same pool that I walked around and around, holding my father's hand, distracting him when he became too agitated to cope with life anymore.

The memories flooded my brain, and I just wasn't prepared for this.

My sister hugged me. Thank God we have each other. Our relationships with our siblings are complicated. They are not like friends who come in and out of our lives or people we have chosen to be with, yet they have always been there. We didn't choose for them to be in our lives, but we are connected from the very beginning. How is it possible to come from the same parents and be so different? We don't even feel like we grew up in the same house, even though we all lived under the same roof. But on that particular day, the three of us, regardless of our differences, were there for the same reason. I hadn't been there since my dad died, since that day when I kissed him goodbye. It was a Thursday. I walked around in circles, crying. My brother said maybe I needed to take a walk, but I knew I would be okay, that I needed to adjust to what I came there to do. We each took on different roles, which I suppose the three of us had always done, but for some reason it became much more obvious that day. My brother and sister told me that I didn't get the "nostalgia gene" because I was able to throw things away easily, while they were busy examining and reminiscing.

Thank God I didn't get that gene because if I had we would probably still be there. We filled what seemed like endless amounts of huge garbage bags. We were even laughing and joking with one another. Then I found the albums, letters, and cards from the life they'd built together. I sat down because I had to. I read letters expressing how they felt about each other. Love letters. They are my parents, but I was seeing a side of them I never knew— their very beautiful love story. It warmed my heart to read them.

Life had become so difficult and sad toward the end of my dad's life, but reading those letters and looking at pictures took away some of the pain that we all endured. They were married almost 57 years, and the last couple of years, as horrific as they were should not define the beautiful life that they built and shared together.

As emotionally wrenching as it was to empty out my mom and dad's apartment, something else happened that day, which I could never have anticipated. I visualized my parents young again and in love. The pictures and letters brought them back to life for me, looking beautiful and happy. I could feel their love for each other.

When someone gets very sick at the end of their life, quite often those memories remain all too vivid, but that day I got to see my mom and dad living life to its fullest, not just the way it was at the end. The pictures told a story of the trips they took all over the world, the parties they made and went to, their friendships, and most important, their family. There are countless pictures of them with their children and grandchildren. Their love for their family was boundless, and a picture *does* tell a thousand words!

The good news is, our parents are living longer than any previous generation. The bad news is, most everyone I know is navigating the uncharted waters of becoming parents to our parents. Most of my friends have at least one parent who they are trying to help have the best quality of life they possibly can, whether they are sick or just need some sort of assistance, or like my mom, make a permanent move.

Whether we are helping them navigate their golden or not so golden years, each of us must figure out how to live our own life the way our heart tells us to, while also telling our mom or dad how they need to live their lives with the hope that it's the right decision. I have friends who are struggling because their relationships with their mom or dad were never good. Now that they need so much care and attention, there is resentment and anger for having to do so much, when they remember that so little was done for them.

We are helping our parents, helping our children, becoming grandparents, and juggling marriage, careers, and friends, but at the end of the day, we all need to place our heads on the pillow and be able to look at ourselves in the mirror the next morning. We must know in our hearts that we did the very best we could do, regardless of how someone else behaved. Peace of mind is the ultimate goal for each and every one of us.

14 *My Mother Has a "Boyfriend"*

It is still difficult for me to say out loud that my mother has a boyfriend. Sydelle and Bob were joined at the hip—Frick and Frack, yin and yang—you get it. They were never without each other for 57 years. That was all any of us had ever known. Everyone loved them and wanted to be around them as a couple because they made you feel good.

My parents opened their home to my friends, who always felt welcome and wanted to be there. We had parties—Sweet 16, engagement, holidays with family, and our home was always buzzing.

Don't get depressed and think my life was one big party. Don't worry, there was plenty of dysfunction to go around. It's not normal if you don't have a little dysfunction. Some just have more than others. We had our share of slamming doors and screaming matches, like all families do. We still talk about the toaster that flew across the backyard! At the end of the day, I believe that if you feel your parents would walk over fire for you, you're going to be just fine. I won't guarantee you won't need a few visits to a therapist, but good luck finding anyone who doesn't.

But, let's get one big thing straight: This is not about me!

When my beloved father died, we were all so consumed in our own sorrow that it was impossible to see anyone else's. When my husband and I took my mom to Florida to settle her back in, we were all in the middle of a blinding snowstorm without windshield wipers, but we did the best we could to help her put one foot in front of another. My husband was a rock. He helped her navigate the bank and lease a car, anything to help her feel as secure as she possibly could at that time.

I had to keep myself together and be strong for my mom. Inside, I was numb. Walking into what had always been their apartment and not seeing my father was too much. Where was he? What happened to all of us? Would we ever be okay again? At the time, I didn't think so, it was so sad.

It was so difficult to say goodbye at the airport, but I knew that for my mother the Florida sun had to be better than the New York snow.

We spoke every day. Mom is a strong woman, but this was uncharted territory for all of us. My father was the captain of their ship and ours as well. Her friends were supportive and caring and she made it through the first storm, the first Florida season without her partner. In April, my sister and I picked her up at the airport, and she looked really good. She agreed to stay at my house for a day or two to acclimate back to New York, afraid to walk into her empty apartment.

The first night, while Mom was upstairs getting ready for bed and Warren and I were in the kitchen, talking and having a glass of wine, we heard her talking. Was she talking to herself? Then we heard laughter. We looked at each other, and realized my mother was on the phone, giggling. Who the hell was she talking to at 11 p.m., let alone giggling like a teenager? Was I in the twilight zone? When she came downstairs, we tried to ask her as nonchalantly as possible.

She told us she had been spending time with a man whose name was Kappy. Kappy, what kind of name is that? When she got down to Florida, a few couples went out to dinner one night and invited my mom and Kappy. Mom doesn't think it was intentional. I didn't agree. As it turned out, Kappy's wife had died shortly after my dad. These were all mutual friends, and it was just a dinner.

He initially called her to see how she was doing. Then they met for coffee, and then dinner, and then a movie, until it became real companionship. They obviously had much in common. They both had just lost their lifetime spouses.

We just sat there and listened. I could hear her words, but it was impossible to process what she was saying. When she spoke about Kappy, she wasn't sad or crying, and that's what mattered. Mom told us it was nice to have the company in Florida, but she really didn't know what would happen because he lived there permanently and she was back in New York until next winter.

Mom settled back in New York and did the best she could. Shortly after her return, she told me Kappy was coming to visit, that he has family here in New York. We were all just following her lead until the next thing we knew, Mom wanted us to meet Kappy. I tried as hard as I could to put my feelings and emotions aside, reminding myself that this was not about me, but it was so surreal. It felt like I was walking in someone else's life. My mom and dad were a team, a unit, a couple. I wasn't able to comprehend one without the other. Who was this man, Kappy, anyway, and what was he doing in my house?

When Mom introduced Kappy to me and Warren we couldn't help but like him, even though I didn't want to. He was warm, friendly and complimentary. Looking back, it must have been so difficult for both of them, as well.

I sat in one chair, Warren in another, and the two of them sat on the couch, together, really together, as in no space between them. They were affectionate with each other, hands on each other's knees, smiling and laughing.

I kept pouring myself another glass of wine when I was supposed to be filling theirs. My mother was being a flirt and so was he. I never had a mother like that. Who was she? And what did you do with my mother? Then again, I never knew my mother and father when they were dating. They were both so open and honest about the gratitude they felt for finding each other and the companionship they were enjoying. They both had been devoted, loving spouses who had spent the last several years of what had been a wonderful life dedicated to the wellbeing of their beloved.

I know that for a fact because I watched my mom's love and devotion, day in and day out, year after year, until the bitter end. "Till death do us part." For me, it will always remain my model of what commitment, love, and devotion should be. Anyone can go to a party, but trust me, this was no party.

I was happy for Mom to see her feeling alive again, to see her smile and look beautiful. That's what I saw when she was with Kappy. When she wasn't with him, the loneliness became, in her words, "excruciating pain."

Kappy flew back and forth from Florida that first summer and gradually met the rest of the family. As much as none of us wanted Mom to be unhappy, everyone adjusted.

"Nana, he's a very nice guy," Daniel said, "but how come so soon?

"Daniel, my darling, I love you more than you can know, but I will be 80 years old very soon. What should I be waiting for?"

"I guess I didn't look at it like that, Nana."

But then my daughter, Jessica said, "You go, Nana, you're like senior Sex in the City!"

Like I said, everyone gets used to things at their own pace, and that's okay.

My mom and Kappy made a wonderful life together. They care about each other and have fun together. It's true companionship.

I still find it difficult to call Kappy my mother's boyfriend. It has absolutely nothing to do with him. We all think he's a wonderful man, and are so grateful that they have each other. There is just a part of me that still cannot believe that my dad is gone forever and I know I will always feel this way.

For those who are living through a similar experience, and I know there are many, be patient and open-minded. Always try and remember that even though you have had a devastating loss, chances are, at the end of the day, you are going home to your partner and not sleeping in an empty bed or eating dinner alone.

We all take the details of our lives for granted, those that are lost and gone forever, when someone dies. As time has passed, I have gained some perspective. For any of you going through this uncharted territory, know that your feelings, whatever they may be, are normal. I couldn't have imagined that I could be writing or talking about my dad without crying. For a long time, I couldn't. But miraculously, now I can. It just happened, and I don't know when, but it did.

As my dad would always say to me, "This too shall pass, and it always does."

15 Back to School, Back to Me

Warren has been traveling for most of our married life. I don't particularly love it, but I've generally learned to accept it. I suppose if I didn't care, what would be the point of staying married? I am grateful that I still feel unhappy and lonely after all these years and would rather have him home than away—most of the time! I try to make the best of my alone time. When my children were young, a.k.a. the "nervous breakdown years," (okay, I can be a bit of a drama queen) it was difficult being alone with a baby and toddler—for me, anyway.

You girls know what I am talking about if you had husbands who were not home, but hopefully, without too much collateral damage, we survived. As my kids got a little older, they became great companions for me. In some ways, life became a little easier as they grew up, and in other ways it became way more difficult.

My son was in college and my daughter was a senior in high school when life as I had only known it was about to take a drastic turn. Not only were both of my children about to be out of the house—my husband was also gone most of the time.

He was worried, and so was I.

Warren expressed his concerns about the changes that were about to occur. He knew that his life was not changing at all. Why is it that their life never seems to change while ours keeps facing one crossroad after another?

I had my own business for several years, which was fulfilling on many levels. It was called The Perfect Present. There were three of us. I was the artist, personalizing children's furniture. One of my partners created beautiful gift baskets, and the other handled invitations and the bookkeeping. We were raising our children during those years, so the business allowed us the flexibility we needed, while at the same time we could be creative and have something else to enjoy. We had the business for several years, with some success. Mostly, it was a great venture and we developed lifelong friendships. I am proud of what we accomplished.

But personally, I needed a change. It was time for me to pursue another career, something totally different than being an artist. I decided to go back to school and become a therapist.

I had thought about doing this for many years but since I was a full-time mother (and part-time father) the thought of it was too overwhelming. Then, the timing seemed just right. All I needed was the courage to take the first step, which is always the hardest.

Was I going to spend the rest of my life like I did the first half, wanting and needing approval from the outside world? I was definitely not about to do that! If someone didn't think I was good enough, who cares? I knew there was one way to go. Put one foot in front of another and you will get where you need to be. You may fall down on occasion, but put your big girl panties on, dust yourself off, and get going!

And that's exactly what I did when I called C.W. Post University, where I had gone to undergraduate school 100 years ago, and made an appointment with an advisor in the Mental Health Counseling Dept. As I drove on to the campus, memories began to flood my mind and nothing seemed to have changed. I even felt young again being there, until I saw students my kids' age, which quickly brought back to the reality that I was a 50-year-old on a campus with 18-year-olds. Ouch! Even so, I felt an inner peace being there, probably because it's where I met the man who I would spend the rest of my life with.

An advisor explained the Mental Health Counseling Masters Program, a 60-credit series of courses I could complete by attending part-time or full-time. I couldn't tell at what point I felt like I was in a doctor's office or when I stopped hearing what she was saying, but I am pretty sure it was when I heard 60 credits. It was quite honestly impossible to imagine being able to complete a program so demanding at that point of my life. I guess the glaze in my eyes became apparent, so we started to talk about my concerns and fears. My reading material basically consisted of *People* magazine and I could not imagine having the ability to comprehend medical journals or writing papers. She suggested that I start with an introductory class. Well, for God sake, I could handle that or at least make believe I could.

I marched myself over to the bookstore after meeting with my advisor. I had an advisor! I purchased a notebook and the book required for the course and couldn't resist a school sweatshirt. Stop laughing. It sort of made me feel young again.

On the ride home, I thought about the fact that I wasn't moving into a dorm, but I would like to create a place just for me, for my new adventure.

When we bought our first house, the one we're still living in 33 years later, my son had just turned two. I decorated his room with blue and white stripes with an adorable animal border. It was all boy! The third bedroom we made into a cozy little den, which we used for the next year a half, until

Jessica arrived and it became a sweet little nursery for our new baby girl.

Whatever improvements we made to our house were always centered around what worked best for our children. It was how we felt about everything. They always came first, and we loved having friends and family around us.

We still do.

Then the years flew by. It's surreal to think about just how old your children are and how old we are, and so fast! Of course we know the facts, but the emotional part just makes it seem impossible sometimes. Okay, enough about that stuff. Let's get to what is really important—me and my space—because it's all about ME!

My kids both moved back home after college for a while and my mother warned me they would. When they were leaving for college and I was crying to her, she would say the same thing again and again.

"Calm yourself down, trust me, they come back and it's not that pretty."

Eventually, they were gone for good and so was their stuff. It was kind of peaceful having the house to ourselves after all these years. Actually, not kind of, it was! I don't think I have to say that I love it when they visit, or even stay over on occasion, and I especially love when they do their food shopping here!

My daughter had been moved out for about 10 minutes when I decided that I needed a room of my own. What, you think I waited too long? My neighbor thought we were selling the house because all her furniture was on the stoop waiting for special pick-up! Don't judge me, I told you I wasn't sentimental, and I have other qualities, but that's just not one of them. I wasn't exactly sure what I was going to do, but I did know that I needed and wanted my own space, just for me and my new college adventure.

I fell in love with an enormous armoire, which Warren felt would never fit into that room. I sort of agreed, but wouldn't admit to that because I had to have it! So what if it had to be cut in half and rebuilt in the room? What, that never was done before? It worked out, they fit it in, and I loved it!

That was my starting point and everything else worked around that. I have black and white striped wallpaper with one wall painted pink. The carpet is a floral design with lots of pink. It is definitely a girl's room and all mine!

I'm probably sounding a little self-absorbed here, and if I want to be truly honest, I was. But when my children moved out to be on their own, it felt like I needed to do something for this new turning point in my life.

From the minute you bring a child into this world, your life as a woman assumes a different meaning and purpose. Everything you do, plan, think, and feel revolves around this tiny little person you have created. Could anything be more daunting than that? You spend many years guiding and loving this child to the very best of your ability. It's a long road, but it's what we will always do—now and forever!

But back to me. I love my space. It's so important, no, I think it's crucial, to figure out something just for you. It doesn't matter what it is, but find something that gives you peace and tranquility. It's crucial to slow down and be alone with yourself. Don't be afraid of the quiet. Embrace it. The solitude will help you appreciate the outside world.

As women, we are pulled in a million directions. Just as our children needed to be weaned from us so that they could become strong, independent people, we need to be weaned from them, as well. We are so conditioned to be part of every aspect of their lives since they were born that even though they are adults now, sometimes the involvement is just as much as when they were little.

For me, it's been a conscious decision to take a few steps back. It's healthier for me, and better for them. When I say a few steps back, I mean, I call less, text less, ask fewer questions, and let them tell me what they want to tell me. It hasn't always been easy making these changes. By nature, I am a yenta and I want to know what they are doing and planning and feeling, but it doesn't make for a healthy, happy adult relationship. Less becomes more.

Although my pink room was a pretty feminine room just for me, it was also the room where I completed my masters program. Something that seemed so unattainable at first became doable because I committed to putting one foot in front of another. That way, I was able to accomplish something I never thought I could.

My pink room has become a metaphor for my life, and hopefully yours, too. When obstacles arise, when problems occur, when the shit hits the fan, I try to remember how I achieved something I really didn't believe I could.

"One foot in front of the other" always eases the anxiety and allowed me to move forward. There are times when we get stuck in yesterday, but there really is only today.

It's so easy to just say, "Well, that's just the way I am and I'm too old to change." It's just not true. We nurture, I get it. But it's really okay, especially now, more than ever, to take care of ourselves. It doesn't mean I've stopped caring or loving; it just means that I'm doing this for myself. When we begin to care for ourselves, we become better at just about everything!

Women tend to overthink, over-analyze and become easily overwhelmed with how we see things, and what we should do next. Many of us live in a "What if?" world and often end up doing nothing when we really want and need to make a change. Fear stops us from taking on challenges, or making changes we know we need to make, even if they are small. Why not choose to welcome change instead of fighting it? Even if it feels uncomfortable and may cause you to be anxious, that doesn't mean it is the wrong decision.

A pink room may not be exactly what you need or want, but I am confident that once you start looking, you are going to find something that's perfect, just for YOU!

We live in a world that's a merry go round. It never stops. Most of the time, it's fun. The sights are pretty, with the wind in your hair, and life is good! Sometimes, you want to get off, and only you can know that. If you pay attention to your mind and body there will be signs. Listen to your inner voice and not the brain chatter. To thine own self be true. You will know when to stay on the merry go round and when it is time to take a break.

With my pink room all to myself, and, with my advisor, notebook, and new college sweatshirt, I began my new adventure. Guess what? I really loved being back in school. The younger people embraced me. They were so kind and helpful, and the others in my age bracket, well we just would looked at each other with that "not sure what we are doing here" look. I took notes like a madwoman, highlighted everything, and loved everything about it.

Mental health was always something I have cared deeply about and I always will.

After completing my first course, I made the decision to commit to the Masters Program to become a Mental Health Therapist. When I felt overwhelmed with the workload, I would come back to the present and not allow myself to obsess over what was ahead of me. I would tell myself that the time is going to pass anyway, and it certainly did. I finished the program in two and a half years and achieved my degree!

For several years, I worked in a psychiatric hospital as a mental health therapist, counseling people and their families struggling with mental illness and addiction. It was an extremely challenging career, but the rewards of feeling that I could help even just one person was far greater for me than any of the day-to-day challenges.

16 A Wedding, A Divorce

My beautiful Jessica became engaged over Labor Day weekend almost two years ago. Every mom dreams of the time her little girl will find a partner for life. The awkward years are long gone, the braces are off, broken hearts are mended, and no more frogs are waiting to be kissed…

Jessica lived in Dallas at the time with her fiancé, which made wedding planning challenging, but nothing we couldn't handle. For me, life was perfect. I was in a fabulous place. My first grandchild was turning one and my daughter was engaged to a wonderful young man from an equally wonderful family. I was feeling so grateful, happy, and fulfilled.

When my father died six years ago, I never imagined my life would be whole again. When Daniel's marriage began to unravel, similar emotions surfaced again. Grieving the loss of my father allowed me to understand the process, and helped me discover that we *can* feel whole and happy while learning to live without him. Once again, I was in uncharted waters, grieving the death of my son's marriage. My father had been sick for a long time, and as painful as it was, his death did not come as a shock. But Daniel's situation felt like a train wreck, a plane crash. No one saw it coming. We had just celebrated my Sloaney's first birthday surrounded by family and friends—one big happy family, one big ugly lie.

It could happen to anyone. I knew all the statistics but until it affects you personally you just don't experience it the way others do. It's not that difficult to understand given the strains any relationship faces. Whether it's difficulties raising children, financial pressure, or health issues. I could go on forever.

Unfortunately, most people don't discuss their struggles, because let's face it, we are not talking about boyfriends, we are talking about husbands, wives, and children. It is sad that people usually wait until it's too late. Maybe at the end of the day, the results would have been the same, but I believe strongly that we all struggle at some point in our marriages—not just once, but many times.

My daughter's engagement party was scheduled for the Saturday of Thanksgiving weekend. We were all brimming with excitement. She deserved every minute of it. Exactly one week earlier, we were slammed in the back of the head with a two by four by Daniel's pending divorce—all of us except the bride to be—we kept that a secret because she deserved her moment in the sun. I continued the lies and the cover up until I thought we had no choice. My daughter-in-law was Jessica's maid of honor. I don't know how we kept everything from Jessica, but we did. We became award-winning actors, at least for a little while. One day at a time, we continued to put on a happy face for the rest of the world, but mostly for my daughter. She and her fiancé returned to Dallas after the party. Life continued, and so did the lies.

It reached a point where it was impossible to keep the secret from her. We didn't have secrets in our family. It was too painful, and she needed to know the truth. But this was Daniel's story to tell, not mine, and so he did. Even though she was in Dallas, she might as well have been on the moon. That's how far away I felt from her and she from us. It was awful, impossible for her to wrap her mind around what was happening. No one in our family could accept what was happening.

Then again, we had no choice. The lies, the cover ups, the acting was over and so was my son's marriage. We all needed to do what was best for him and our family, and for my beautiful, precious Sloane.

How exactly does one plan a wedding and a divorce at the same time? It felt like I was driving in a relentless, blinding snowstorm with broken windshield wipers. I knew how to be part of a family and love my children. I knew that whatever happens in a family, you support each other and to the best of your ability you become part of the solution, regardless of how overwhelming the problems may be. You fight with everything you have. Apparently, not everyone sees family that way.

But I had a wedding to plan. In between the dark days, I had the joy of shopping for my daughter's gown, something every mom fantasizes about. I was able to compartmentalize my emotions during those special times with Jessica on her trips to New York. I could watch, as my little girl became the most exquisite vision right before my eyes. She brought me so much joy, and I was so happy for her. As difficult as it was for her living so far away, I think it was a blessing in disguise. She and her fiancé needed that time together to build their foundation. It was just the two of them, and even though she knew what was happening, she wasn't living it 24/7 like we were. I wanted her to have a happy engagement. Every girl deserves that!

As a society, we are so insistent upon early intervention with our health. I wonder if that approach could help relationships, as well. I tend to think so.

Getting married is not the hard part, but staying married is. You must always compromise, and who the hell wants to do that? You are two totally different people living under the same roof. There are plenty of times when you want to scream "Get your own Goddamn roof to live under" and you probably have, and will again, but you stay together. You've built a life; you are committed to one another, and you love each other. As long as you keep the window to your heart open, everything and anything is possible.

Daniel began the process of rebuilding his life brick by brick, never missing a beat with his beautiful Sloane. We continued to be the best support we could while searching for florists, photographers and bands. Jessica and Ross moved back to New York in the fall, a perfect time to continue planning their springtime wedding, when we could finally be a family once again and begin the process of creating our new normal.

Daniel needed me for many things and I needed to be there for him. Jessica needed me, too, and the guilt was overwhelming and tearing me apart. A pending divorce and an upcoming wedding. It wasn't fair. What happened to the life I had? I was doing the best I could, but it never seemed enough. I tried to hide my pain when I was with Jessica. The last thing I wanted to do was be a burden, but her heart was hurting, too, for her brother and her family.

Day by day, we grew stronger. That's the power of real love.

The wedding was *perfect* in every way. Jessica and Ross glowed all night, and their love and devotion to each other shines through in every photograph. Sloane was a precious flower girl, marching down the aisle barefoot. My mom, Jessica's Nana, danced at her granddaughter's wedding and Daniel looked more handsome than ever as he walked her down the aisle. I was bursting with love and pride, surrounded by my family and friends.

Your days may turn very dark and I don't know exactly when or how, but slowly, day-by-day, the light begins to shine through and the darkness begins to fade. I now know for sure that the best is yet to come.

17 Dance of a Marriage

So the kids are grown and out of the house, off the payroll (sort of), and everyone's getting a little older, feeling the need to "smell the roses" as time seems to move faster and faster. Some of us are talking retirement, while others just take more time for travel or whatever it was they put on hold while building careers and raising families. Here we are once again, entering another chapter of our lives, which some refer to as the "sometimes too much time together" chapter!

It seems that women have always been able to juggle and reinvent themselves. Many men have been defined solely by their career, with not much time for anything else. Women are usually the ones who make the plans that keeps the merry go round moving.

Most of our conversations as a married couple were about the kids, the dog, and of course "stop spending so much money!" These days, we still talk about the same topics (except the dog) but just not as much. It's me and you, staring at each other, and while we've been juggling and reinventing ourselves every ten minutes, they want to know what's for lunch. Now what?

I can't believe he said that.

Why does he always do that?
Doesn't he know how that makes me feel?
After all these years, shouldn't he know better?
Is there anything new under the sun?
I remember my father's advice when I got married.

"Honey, don't fool yourself into thinking you will be changing anybody. The good gets better and figure out if you can deal with the not so good. Just make sure the good outweighs the bad."

So not much has really changed at all. I wonder about the couples I know and why some marriages endure while others do not. Obviously, none of us are privy to what's going on behind closed doors and we can't always understand the challenges others face being married and staying married.

Some just don't make it. Experiencing the divorce of our long-time best friends was devastating. We shared everything—holidays, Bar Mitzvahs and Bat Mitzvahs, family vacations, and travelling around the world. We tried to the best of our ability to be supportive friends, but the life that we had known for so long began to unravel and we entered unfamiliar territory, not sure how to navigate our own emotions with the parents and children. We loved them both, but I could hardly understand what was going on myself, let alone explain it to my children.

We remained friends for as long as we could. There was little to do other than listen to their pain, but the marriage was over. The life we had shared together was over, too, and it felt like someone had died.

There is a time to grieve for the life we had shared together and we spent time talking to our children to help them feel secure and safe in the aftershock of what felt like a domestic earthquake.

I hope that many years later, both of them and their kids have found peace.

Having the ability to reinvent oneself is crucial. You

cannot imagine in the moment how you will be able to do it, but as it turns out, you have the strength and resiliency you never knew existed until you were put to the test. Give yourself the gift of time to heal.

The heart mends. Be receptive. New people will come into your life only if the window to your heart and mind stay open. I know how much easier it is to live with your window shut tight. It feels safer, and you don't have to worry that something unfamiliar will fly in. But if you choose that option, you will spend the rest of your days missing out on a beautiful butterfly or a precious ladybug meant to enter your life!

Perhaps staying married is like going on a diet. Anyone can lose weight, but it's how you sustain the loss that really matters. There are setbacks along the way, when you want to eat an entire pizza by yourself or drive through McDonald's and supersize everything, but most likely, even though you want to, you don't. Chances are, you talk yourself through it, have a good fight, make up, and settle for a cookie or two or three…

So it continues, the dance of a marriage. He says this, you say that, he makes you laugh, you make him angry, you give him space, he pisses you off, you say something stupid, he doesn't listen. The dips, the swirls, the back step, the miss step—it's the pas de deux the two of you do. Sometimes you're in sync and you feel like Ginger Rogers and Fred Astaire. Sometimes the music is too fast or too slow and you just don't want to dance. What I've come to understand after all of these years is that if you stay the course and choose to weather the storms you will find that nothing lasts forever; there will always be another song, and you will be ready to dance again.

Marriage is similar to childbirth and raising children. If you knew everything you would have to endure, I am not sure we would all be signing up so quickly, but for better and for worse, it's been one amazing ride.

Warren and I met in college during our senior year. I knew right away that he was the one for me, and I informed him that I was definitely the one for him! We were engaged and married within the year. I couldn't take a chance that he would change his mind, could I? I know it sounds cliché but I remember life being so much easier back then. We both worked. I was in the city, and he was on Long Island. How could I have known that those first years would be the foundation we continued to build our marriage on?

Now I understand that if your foundation is not strong from the beginning, chances are when the winds begin to blow and the blinding snowstorms fall (and trust me, they do) your marriage may not weather the storm.

You start a family, you both juggle careers, experience financial gains and setbacks, face the challenges of aging parents, and maintain relationships with friends and each other. After each storm, you dust off and reflect back on the life you built together with this other person, the one you married a long time ago and could not imagine ever being without.

You get on each other's nerves, and doors slam, and sometimes you don't fight fair. I never understood what the heck that meant anyway because you still say things that demand an apology and sometimes you really don't get each other, which really pisses me off, even after all these years. I still get the same shopping questions about my clothes and shoes, but I accept that I always will. How mature of me!

Speaking of clothes and shoes (and what girl doesn't), I was in fifth grade when I first fell in love with Paris. Well, I actually fell in love with the French language because my French teacher, who was so beautiful, looked like Audrey Hepburn, which probably wasn't true, but I'm sticking with that memory. She looked even prettier when she spoke French and I got a French award that year. At 10 years old, my future was set. I would become a French teacher and look just like her. Well, let's just say I never became a French teacher, I am not tall, and I'm still working on the other part!

Becoming a French teacher wasn't in the cards for me, even though I never stopped dreaming that one day I would get to Paris. After studying art history, my dreams of Paris grew larger. I fantasized about actually seeing it up close and not just in movies or books.

Years passed, and still no Paris. We took other amazing trips to Europe, all of which I loved, but no Paris—that is, until last November, when Warren and I spent two weeks driving all over France. To be honest, I was a little worried about traveling that long without any other friends. Most of our trips had been with at least one other couple and you know what that means. You speak to your husband at the airport and then again in the car coming home.

The last time we traveled alone was on our honeymoon, when I was cute and thin and thought everything he did and said was sweet and funny and nothing about my husband got on my nerves!

Oy vey! What did I get myself into? Would there be anything to talk about after we got off an eight-hour plane ride and the wine wore off? I was quite sure we had discussed everything! But I was pleasantly surprised. It really was a wonderful, romantic time and one of my favorite trips. We ate and drank what and when we wanted. There wasn't anyone else to discuss anything and agree with and we talked and we didn't and it didn't matter. We did whatever we wanted. It was reassuring to know that after so many years of being married we still could spend so much time together—alone.

Paris didn't disappoint me either. I loved everything about it. I knew I would. My feelings about being in another country are similar to being a guest in someone's home. You need to be gracious, respectful, and well-mannered. Although there are so many differences in our cultures, everyone, no matter what language, color, or nationality they claim, will always be receptive to a kind word. When we were in Italy, I knew one word, "molto bene," and no matter when or where I said it, a smile came back every time. In France, I remembered some of my French from 100 years ago and when I was in a store (when wasn't I?), I would say "très, très jolie," and again, always a smile.

Paris is charming and beautiful, especially at night. Their attention to detail is impeccable and everyone seems to have a stunning sense of style. We drove through much of the French countryside, staying in small little towns along the way to Provence, a part of the world where I could have easily stayed much longer. The simplicity and the pace were so appealing. People shopped at local outdoor markets and the shops were so beautiful. I felt like I had lived there before and even experienced a spiritual connection being there, as silly as that may sound. Perhaps for those two weeks, I was that little girl in fifth grade again, falling in love with a country, its language and its people!

Maybe inside each one of us a little girl still remains, even after we get married, have children, build careers, lose parents, and become mothers-in-law and grandmothers. Maybe dreams that never materialized can come alive, even if it is just for two weeks.

Warren and I didn't fight, argue about nonsense, or get on each other's nerves. For two whole weeks, I never saw "the look." Stop it, you know the look, the one that says, "I'm not exactly sure how I got here and now what did I do wrong?" And don't talk to me about money! I'm not sure if they are genetically predisposed or if it's something they have developed throughout years of being married. Don't pretend you don't know what I'm talking about. We all know "the look."

My husband's favorite joke is, "Why do Jewish men die young? Because they want to."

I get it. "We" aren't always easy-breezy.

He told me I should design Jewish husband flashcards and hold them up so he can be sure and say exactly what I need to hear. Isn't that brilliant? But the truth is, all of this really doesn't matter. The only thing that I care about is that the two of us built our foundation brick by brick a long time ago and because we built it with love and respect for one another, we have been able to weather the storms that have come in and out of our lives. We are sure to face more obstacles but there isn't anyone else I could ever imagine growing old with and I hope he feels the same. If he doesn't, I will hold up the Jewish husband flashcard so he'll know just what I need him to say.

18 *Learning to Live Without You*

April 5, 2011

Dearest Dad,

Happy Anniversary. It would have been 59 years today that you and Mom were married. I can hear you saying, "That's a number."

Mom is doing pretty well since you've been gone. I know in my heart you would want that for her. She spends most of her time with Kappy. Mom said you knew him and his wife from Century Village but didn't socialize in the same circle. I teased Mom from the beginning that I was sure you sent Kappy to her because you knew she could not be alone and you wanted her to be happy. I also told her I'm pretty sure you were really happy that someone else was paying! She always laughs when I say that.

Today, Warren and I are driving to Fort Lauderdale to see Mom and Kappy. He is a great companion for her. Don't be jealous! You know there isn't anyone on this earth who could hold a candle to you, but he cares about Mom.

Two things he does have on you is that he is punctual and a good listener. That's according to Mom. In my eyes, you were the greatest father—pretty close to perfection!

Mom has finally come to terms with moving to Florida permanently. It's been a grueling decision for her, especially because she said your words still haunt her. She knows how adamant you were about keeping your home in New York to be close to your children, but our family dynamics have changed dramatically since you're gone. It's not only because of your absence, although I am sure that plays a huge part. Maybe you were the glue that kept us together or maybe it's just that nothing stays the same. Maybe it's the way life is supposed to be right now, and we are all better off coping with the changes rather than living in the past.

Warren and I are doing really well. He misses you so much, Dad. He misses talking to you and hearing all the confidence you had in him. He works really hard, traveling all over. You were a dad to him in every sense of the word.

One of my favorite stories I love to tell about your relationship with Warren is when he was at the airport, waiting for a flight with someone from Italy. Warren's phone rang, and it was you, wishing him a good trip. You always did that! You and Warren chatted for a while, and said goodbye.

"You are so lucky that your dad is still living," The man told Warren.

"That wasn't my father; it was my father-in-law."

Your love was so abundant.

Warren and I have been married for 38 years now. He did take up golf, which I know you would have been happy about. You and mom played in Florida, and loved it. We are playing golf together at a country club we joined, and sometimes when I play I think of you and how happy you would be for us. I wish I could share the club with you. Oh yes, we are very fancy! You would be so proud; you always were, no matter what we were doing or where we were going. I would bring you to "Seafood Night" so you could eat as much lobster and shrimp as you wanted. When I close my eyes, I can still see you loving it!

Here we are, driving to Fort Lauderdale, after spending a weekend in Marco Island. I love the beach, and I get that from you. You loved the beach so much. It reminded me of Ocean City, with all the young families. We had the best times there. One day, we will be back there with our own grandchildren.

Everyone in the family is doing well, finding their place in the world. We stay connected as best we can, and you can be sure we will always be there for one another.

Dad, I miss you so much. I think about you every single day, and many nights I dream about you. I know you are gone, but I still have so much trouble grasping that I won't see you again. I look at your pictures and always wonder where did you go?

I miss your guidance more than you can know, your excitement, your interest in all the details of our lives, your confidence in me when I was feeling lost. You gave me many gifts in my lifetime. So many of my behaviors and beliefs are like yours. Some would say that means you are always with me. I suppose there is some truth to that, but then again, they didn't have a father like you. Nobody I knew did.

I still expect you to come barreling through my front door with your tail wagging and your open arms with a big kiss, always telling me how beautiful I am. Imagine a world where every father treats his daughter like that. I'm pretty sure I am set for life because of your love and devotion. But the hole in my heart can never be filled. It's just not possible, and I am learning to accept that and to live each day without you.

I always remember your words to live by:

Think about it in the morning. Everything looms so large and ugly at night.

Write it down, figure out a timetable when to revisit and re-evaluate.

Every pot has a cover.

What goes around comes around, usually worse.

Relationships are all about balancing the good and bad. Just know that the good gets better and the bad gets worse. Only you can decide what you can live with.

The most important:

This, too, shall pass.

My beloved father, we are all healthy and making our own way. We have a really good life. I try to be grateful for all that I have. Sometimes, I see my glass half full, but mostly I am happy and know that all you ever wanted was to make sure your family was well taken care of and happy. So far, so good. The seeds you and mom planted a long time ago have now yielded a beautiful garden. Because you taught me so well, I am watching and watering my garden, and just like you, I will never stop.

I love you, forever and always.

19 *Mirror, Mirror, on the Wall*

Are you doing anything special for your 60th? A party, a trip, amazing jewelry? How does it feel turning 60? Are you depressed? Can you believe it? How is it even possible? You look really good for 60! Really? What does that mean, anyway? What did I look like *before* 60?

First of all, why the big hoopla? It's just a number, and it means nothing, kind of like the number on a scale. I'm not particularly happy about it, and yes it is difficult at times to wrap my mind around it, but do I really want to obsess and ruin the rest of my days ruminating about a number that continues to inch up? I try to change the things I can and accept the things I can't. However, if "the husband" is experiencing a little jewelry guilt over me turning 60, I would never want to be responsible for taking that away from him.

Is 60 the new 40? *Absolutely not*! Who in their right mind wants to go back to a time when life was all about kids? Enough of that already! Do you really want to go back to a daily obsession about your thighs or other body parts you hated? Our clothes fit better. We didn't need to color our hair every three weeks or keep five pairs of readers in every pocketbook. Spanx was not in my vocabulary or in my closet. Still, I don't think it was necessarily a better time.

People often tend to romanticize their younger years. Remember this; remember that. We all do it. Sometimes it's fun to reminisce, but it's healthier to embrace wherever you are right now. Personally, I've come to think that these are our golden years right about now!

It's normal to have all of these thoughts and feelings and no one dies from having them. It's okay to feel angry, sad, happy, or lonely. Embrace your feelings. Give yourself permission to be a human being.

For the most part I wouldn't trade this time for any other. It's all about accepting what is, not what you thought it was going to be. Our lives turn left when we think they will go right, and most of the time there weren't any maps or a GPS to show us the way. But somehow I got here. In fact, most of us have had to create our own personal GPS to navigate the ups and downs of our own personal journey.

Here's what I love about turning 60.

I have been married to the same person for 40 years and I have no regrets. I accept that he and I are different, and that he is not changing a single hair on his head (he still has some). We have built a strong, beautiful life together and I hope we will be given the gift of growing old together.

My children are all grown up. I love being with them— not because they are my children, but because I love being with the people they have become.

My mom and I are great friends. I accept her as a human being, with flaws like the rest of us. I treasure that no one in this world could love me more.

My beloved father isn't here physically, but I treasure his memory and know that he is with me every single day.

My friends are those I *choose* to keep. It no longer matters if they have a child in my daughter's class or if their son plays soccer. We are sharing *our* lives now.

At 60, less is more.

I try to stay away from the "what if" world, a place that fills us with anxiety and keeps us up all night. It is incredible how nothing we worry about actually happens. Instead, it's usually something we never saw coming! I try to avoid spending my time worrying about what I cannot control.

Last, but not least—me. I feel free. Free to be me, and if you like me, great. I am doing the best I can, and at 60, I know I am good enough.

There are still times I would like to hit my husband with a frying pan but it's much less than before. Now I have the ability to walk away, zip up my big mouth, and talk about "it" later.

I am not as thin as I would have hoped, and still feel guilty when I indulge in a slice of pizza, but I am not relentless about it. I am kinder to myself now. I have patience, compassion, perspective, and even wisdom.

So 60, here I am! Not every day, not every minute, but for the most part, it's a peaceful time. I hope and I pray good health will continue to be a gift given to all those I love, cherish, and treasure.

20 *All By Myself, and I'm Okay*

I thought this day would never come.

It's April something and, frankly, I could care less what day it is. I am sitting alone by the pool at a beautiful hotel in Orlando while Warren is finishing up at a tile show. Saying "Good-bye, have a good trip" has always been part of our life together. Now that those two people who used to live with us—the kids—have moved out, I sometimes tag along on some of his trips. For years, it was impossible for me to envision this day. I don't mean to come across as a drama queen (although I have my moments), but I know that those of you in the sisterhood of traveling husbands, you simply get it.

When Warren and I met 100 years ago he was not a traveling salesman. If he had been, even as cute as he was, I would not have gotten involved with him. I just wasn't that carefree kind of independent girl. My parents were my role models, where the husband worked, the wife raised the children, and you had dinner every night as a family when "Daddy" got home from work. It was the 1950's, and in my world husbands and wives did everything together. They may have had their separate card nights, but that was about as separate as life got in the world I grew up in.

There wasn't a girl's night out or girl getaways. That was just the way it was—for me, anyway.

The life I was living did not follow the model of married life I knew. We had been married for about two months when Warren came home one night with exciting news. He had been offered a promotion in his company. How wonderful and exciting! My nice Jewish husband was really stepping up.

One small problem. The job was in California. We had to move! Are you crazy? What did you say? I needed a drink, but I wasn't drinking wine back then. Big mistake! Didn't he realize I was still attached to my mother's umbilical cord? It didn't matter that I had just walked down the aisle two months earlier. I wasn't terribly independent. Believe it or not—because I couldn't—my father sat me down to talk.

"Honey, your husband is beginning his career and they don't ask twice. You need to do this."

My father, who loved and cherished me, had the wisdom, strength, and insight to place his emotions aside and guide me to begin my journey alongside my husband. I was 22 years old. I could not see what he could see and knew to be right.

We packed; we said our goodbyes, and off we went. We drove across the country for two weeks, and although it was an amazing trip, I cried in every state. Looking back, I am surprised Warren didn't leave me in Montana. Hard to imagine, but there weren't any cell phones or computers. We couldn't text one another about the events of the day or just to say I love you. All of the technology we take for granted didn't exist yet. You made phone calls from a pay phone, and if the line was busy you hung up and tried again on another one. There wasn't even a machine to leave a message. We wrote letters and visited once a year.

As I reflect back on that time of our lives, despite how lonely I was, it was probably the best thing that could have happened to me. My father was right. He always was.

When I was in middle school and praying for a boyfriend, he would talk to me about dating. Never about sex! He would get embarrassed and turn various shades of red.

How different things are today. We probably talk to our kids too much, and know too much. But dating, that was different (in his eyes). If I met someone and he didn't think he was "right" for me, he would say, "There is no such thing as a first date."

Of course, I would roll my eyes and get angry. I was a teenager. Didn't he realize I had been praying for a boyfriend? Back then, I didn't have a clue. He felt that if you went out with someone, even one time, two things would happen. If you didn't have a good time, you wouldn't go again, but if you did enjoy yourself, of course you would go again, and again, and again. He felt that you just shouldn't go in the first place if the boy was not "right." Of course I continued to think he was wrong and being too controlling.

Enter children—my own children—and suddenly he was completely right.

Don't you just hate it when you realize just how many things your parents were right about?

In any case, I learned to turn to my husband instead of my parents, and we began building our foundation together, one that has remained intact despite weathering many a storm. Living far away forced me to begin the difficult journey to becoming independent and it did *not* come naturally to me.

About two years later, we came back to New York, and in case you're wondering, I finally stopped crying. Oy vey! Pretty soon after that, we started our family. Daniel was born and life was good. I was surrounded by family and friends. I was able to stay home with Daniel, which most of my friends, if not all, were doing back then. Don't forget, this was almost 35 years ago.

We were happy back in New York and the furthest

Warren traveled was to New Jersey, which meant he was home every night and everything had returned to the life I had known—until it wasn't.

Shortly after we came back to New York, an opportunity presented itself for Warren to have his own business. Up until then, he had been working for someone else, but this was an opportunity to make more money and build something of his own. Of course when you decide to go out on your own there are huge risks involved, but I trusted and believed in him. He told me that this new venture was going to require "some travel." I didn't think much of it at the time because I didn't know what "some travel" meant. I had never lived that life while growing up because my dad, who was home every night, was a huge part of our day-to-day lives.

We moved into our first and only house. Our daughter, Jessica, was born about a year and a half later, and Warren's traveling began to increase, along with my anxiety, anger, and loneliness. I did not know how to do this alone. I did not *want* to do this alone. My parents were supportive but they were both working full-time. My friends' husbands were home every night, and then there was me, with a toddler and an infant.

It was a very difficult time in our lives. Warren was working extremely hard to make a life for us, and I was working really hard taking care of two babies. I was angry and resentful, which usually doesn't make for a happy relationship.

Jessica was an infant, Daniel was three, and I was sick as a dog with some virus while Warren was away—again. Are you sensing a nervous breakdown approaching? Well, that was the beginning of the nanny/housekeeper revolving door. I hated (I know that's a strong word) having someone living in my house, but at that time, I didn't feel I had a choice. It was either have some help or have a nervous breakdown! Looking back, I'm pretty sure I had both.

Perhaps someone else could have handled my situation better than I did, but my coping skills for raising children alone were not good. I suppose I had never had the need to develop them, and being independent was not one of my stronger traits back then.

Warren was home on weekends, but the more success he had, the more he traveled. He loved what he did and was very good at it. If he weren't on the road, there would be no paycheck. We just never lived the "nine to five get a paycheck every two weeks" kind of life. Over the past 40 years, I have come to understand and accept that fact, and I know he never will.

When problems arise, there aren't always answers, but having someone to share in your angst is quite often all that is needed. Someone to talk you off the ledge, off the roof, or just a hug telling you that everything will be okay.

We all sacrificed something. Early on, I had to make a decision for myself. I could choose divorce because this life was just too difficult for me, or I could fight the fight and learn how to accept the cards I had been dealt. I decided to accept my situation because Warren was worth it, and he still is. He has always been a wonderful and devoted husband and father, providing an incredible life for all of us.

During my nervous breakdown years, something amazing began to happen that I never could have imagined. I was morphing into an independent woman right before my eyes. I am the first to admit that it was not by choice, that's for sure. However, I did know that if I was going to survive, I needed to create my own life, separate from my husband. I needed to learn how to depend on myself.

My girlfriends became a huge support network and I learned that it wasn't a sign of weakness to ask for help. I learned to have dinner alone and not be lonely. I learned that it was okay to go on trips with my girlfriends. I learned how to travel alone and even though I felt anxious I did it anyway. I learned how to stand on my own two feet, and if my husband is next to me I'm really happy, but if he's not, I can still be happy.

A lifetime commitment doesn't come with a lifetime guarantee of happiness. Marriage is difficult, challenging, and frustrating, and some marriages just don't make it through the storms. But for those of us who are in it for the long haul, a successful marriage means putting your boxing gloves away, going a little deaf and accepting your differences. I'm not saying you have to like it; just understand that it's never been all that different. Ultimately, you and only you are responsible for your own happiness

There is no one I know, absolutely no one, who at some point of their life has not been lost in a rainstorm without windshield wipers. Those are the times when we must seek guidance, friendship, or whatever or whoever will help you through. You may feel like you are the only one going through something, but trust me, you are not.

Everyone carries at least one burden, if not more. You must find the strength to have the courage to reach out. If that is too difficult, then let someone in. Whatever path you have walked, give yourself a voice. I promise someone will be listening.

Take a deep breath; count to 10, and of course, a little wine never hurt anyone!

21 The Room at the Top of the Stairs

Mom is visiting from Florida for Thanksgiving to spend time with her children, grandchildren, and great grandchildren. Wow! I hope I have what she has someday. She is upstairs, sleeping in what was originally a small, cozy den, which became a beautiful nursery for my baby girl and continued to be Jessica's room until she moved out.

Our kids are so funny. They are eager to be independent and separate from us, but something happens when they come back to visit. It almost seems like they get upset or insulted when we change something.

"When did you get that? Something looks different."

Maybe they feel we should leave their room like a shrine? Absolutely not. I need more closets for my shoes.

"Don't touch anything. Don't go through my things. There's no space for me."

So what would you like me to do with your Little League trophies and photo albums from sleep-away camp? Wait a minute, you moved out! I didn't!

Jessica's room became my pink room, just for me, and remained my space for quite some time until my Sloaney arrived. Once again, there was a crib and a changing table. I shared my pink room with my girl for a few years until my little angel boy Ethan was born and my pink room morphed into a full-blown children's room once again.

This time it's half pink and half blue. My space became their space! I didn't need my pink room as much as I used to. I need them more.

But this Thanksgiving, their great-grandmother is sleeping here for the weekend. These days when my mom comes to visit, the room at the top of the stairs is not only where my daughter grew up and my grandchildren sleep. It's where my mom sleeps as well, and these dynamics are new for her and all of us.

Mom's boyfriend, Kappy, passed away this past August. He had been sick, but the pain of the loss and the loneliness continue for her. I watch her struggle to reinvent herself at 86 years old. It seems so unfair and cruel. I try to find words to ease her sadness but they feel empty and meaningless.

I just can't imagine. How could I? I haven't walked a minute in her shoes—those of a woman blessed with two wonderful and caring men—my father for 57 years and her companion, her boyfriend, for eight. Together, that makes 65 years of never being alone and having someone to love and care about.

She's never been alone in her adult life until now. Even though my dad was sick for several years, and Kappy was sick for the last year of his life, she still never thought of herself as alone, even though she was. Regardless of the situation, she had someone to love and care for, and that love and devotion ruled the day.

Mom is very independent, sharp as a tack, and looks amazing, but I worry about her, probably the same way she worried about me over the years, wanting to take away my pain but feeling helpless because she couldn't.

Our roles have now reversed. Is that the circle of life? When we are young, we don't worry about our parents. At least I didn't. We are enmeshed in our own lives, raising our children, working, and juggling a variety of things. Our parents shared in our lives, but I don't remember worrying about them. They had each other, and even if there were things to worry about, they never let on. Not in my world, anyway.

Today is uncharted territory once again for us. Mom is doing the best she can and I admire her strength, that she doesn't allow anything to stop her, in spite of feeling fearful and anxious. She flies alone, takes care of her car, and the occasional broken television. She's even on Facebook!

Mothers and their daughters—that could actually be my next book. Where does one even begin to describe the complicated relationship between the two? The push, the pull, the need for acceptance and independence at the same time, the power of words that seem to stay etched in our brains, the yearning for their love who some give so willingly while others are not capable. There are genes we are proud to inherit and others we choose to reject. Mothers who always show up with open arms and hearts and those who don't. Mothers who didn't get the chance to have this complicated relationship because they were taken away all too soon.

Day by day, my mom, who showed up throughout my entire life with open arms and an open heart, continues to reinvent herself. I would give anything to see her happy again. She doesn't burden anyone and puts on a happy face, but she doesn't fool me. She doesn't have to. Just like in my times of sadness, I could never fool her, either. She has always been there for me, and I will always be there for her—and so will the room at the top of the stairs.

Acknowledgments

As with any journey you embark upon, there are many people who become part of that adventure, some just passing through while others remain in it for the long haul. Regardless, this book has been a true labor of love and I would like to acknowledge and thank the people who have been along for the ride.

David Tabatsky, my editor, believed in my project from the first day we met. He respected my vision and guided me through this entire process. I am grateful for his patience, guidance, and the laughs. And thanks to Bruce Kluger, for his creative collaboration.

My family, no matter what, when, or why, always show up, no questions asked.

A huge thank you to all of my girlfriends (and a few men) who laughed and encouraged me every step of the way, beginning with when I told them the title. See you at my book signing!

My Daniel and Jessica, I couldn't cherish or treasure anyone more, and you have given me Sloane and Ethan, the greatest joys I have ever known in my entire life.

Warren, although you continue to roll your eyes when I come up with a new plan, you have always supported me in every venture I have taken, never disappointing me, and always proud of my accomplishments. Forty years this May 13th, and I already have lots of ideas for the next 40!

About the Author

Gayle Israel is an artist and mental health therapist. Her interests include art and travel, but the highlight of her life is spending time with her grandchildren, Sloane Emilie and Ethan Ryan. She lives on Long Island with her husband, Warren.

For more information about this book,
please visit Gayle online:

WEBSITE: www.GayleIsrael.com
INSTAGRAM: @gayleisrael_
FACEBOOK: Gayle Israel Author

Made in the USA
Middletown, DE
26 July 2018